CITYSPOTS
LISBON

Louise Pole-Baker

Written by Louise Pole-Baker
Original photography by Christopher Holt
Front cover photography © Greg Elms/Lonely Planet Images
Series design based on an original concept by Studio 183 Limited

Produced by Cambridge Publishing Management Limited
Project Editor: Jenni Rainford
Layout: Julie Crane
Maps: PC Graphics
Transport map: © Communicarta Limited

Published by Thomas Cook Publishing
A division of Thomas Cook Tour Operations Limited
Company Registration No. 1450464 England
PO Box 227, Unit 18, Coningsby Road
Peterborough PE3 8SB, United Kingdom
email: books@thomascook.com
www.thomascookpublishing.com
+44 (0)1733 416477
ISBN-13: 978-1-84157-634-3
ISBN-10: 1-84157-634-4

First edition © 2006 Thomas Cook Publishing
Text © 2006 Thomas Cook Publishing
Maps © 2006 Thomas Cook Publishing
Series Editor: Kelly Anne Pipes
Project Editor: Ross Hilton
Production/DTP: Steven Collins

Printed and bound in Spain by GraphyCems

CONTENTS

SYMBOLS & ABBREVIATIONS

The following symbols are used throughout this book:

ⓐ address　ⓣ telephone　ⓕ fax　ⓔ email　ⓦ website address
ⓞ opening times　ⓝ public transport connections　ⓘ important

The following symbols are used on the maps:

🛈 information office		○ city	
✈ airport		○ large town	
➕ hospital		○ small town	
🚓 police station		═ motorway	
🚌 bus station		─ main road	
🚆 railway station		─ minor road	
Ⓜ metro		─ railway	
✝ cathedral			
❶ numbers denote featured cafés & restaurants			

Hotels and restaurants are graded by approximate price as follows:
£ budget　££ mid-range　£££ expensive

▶ *A view uphill – Rua do Alecrim*

INTRODUCING
Lisbon

Introduction

Portugal's capital and the country's largest city, Lisbon is an exciting place to visit because of both its sense of history and culture, and its forward-thinking mentality. This sense of history is apparent in its architecture, museums and musical and written culture. Built on seven hills, the most apparent one is crowned by Castelo de São Jorge (see pages 74–6) and is historically and architecturally a reminder of the reclamation of the city from the Moors. At the other end of the city, the 1960s Padrão dos Descobrimentos is a monument to its maritime glories (see page 99). The *azulejos* (Portuguese decorative tiles) seen in palaces, on the sides of houses and the metro, reflect social and cultural history in their style and development. The opulent style of the palaces harks back to the wealth squandered by the royal family and ruling classes, whilst the ruins of the Convento do Carmo and the Baixa Pombalina are reminders of the 1755 earthquake, and the destruction and rebuilding of the city (see page 58).

The 25 de Abril bridge and the modern Ponte de Vasco da Gama – the longest bridge in Europe – link their most famous maritime hero to the modernising European city that it is today.

Large parts of Lisbon's architectural landscape have been transformed since its transition to democracy, from the contemporary building and walkways of the Centro Cultural de Belém (see pages 101–2) to the ambitious Parque das Nações (see pages 110–18), where everything is named after heroes from the past. The city landscape continues to evolve with the addition of new projects by Alvaro Siza, Frank Gehry, Norman Foster, Jean Nouvel and Renzo Piano.

Located at the mouth of the Tagus, there is a rich gastronomy influenced by the sea (see pages 24–7) and the weather is pleasant but cooled by the sea breeze. If it does get hot, though, you can escape to the resorts of the Estoril coastline (see pages 120–31) or seek out cultural delights and shaded parks in Sintra (see pages 132–42). Or just immerse yourself in the fado music (see page 18) of Lisbon's historic Bairro Alto or the nightlife of Alcântara.

⬤ A ferry ride is a great way to enjoy the River Tagus

When to go

SEASONS & CLIMATE

Located at the mouth of the River Tagus (Río Tejo), Lisbon's southerly position gives it a Mediterranean feel, though there are around 100 rainy days a year. The river and Atlantic mean it's not quite as hot here as in the Algarve or inland. Although the average temperature from May to September is 20°C, in July and August this can rise to 30°C or more. The proximity of the river and the sea means there is some breeze but this might be the best time to escape to your hotel swimming pool to cool off. On the other hand, the average temperature from October to April might only be 10°C, but it rarely drops below 5°C, and you can expect a mixture of rainy and sunny days when the sky is an impenetrable blue.

ANNUAL EVENTS

There's a lot going on in Lisbon. To help you to find out what takes place and where, here are some events and festivals. It's a good idea to check with the tourist information office when you're planning your visit.

February

February is **Carnival** time with colourful festivities leading up to Lent. In Lisbon it takes on a particularly Brazilian feel with carnival floats, fancy dress and dancing.

March

Lisbon shakes off its new-year blues with a **Half Marathon** that sees thousands of athletes running along through the Parque das Nações. The Belém Cultural Centre (CCB) hosts its **Spring Festival** with classical music performances, traditional crafts, and flower and fruit market.

May

Big-name bands come to the city for the **Superbock Superrock** rock festival at the Tejo Park. For sporting action head to the Estádio Nacional for the **Estoril Open Tennis Championships** – if you don't manage to get tickets for the main competition there might be tickets for the qualifying rounds. For quite a spectacular sight, take an organised day trip to Fátima for the anniversary of the first apparition of Mary.

June

The streets of the Bairro Alto, Chiado, Baixa and Alfama come alive for the **Festas de Lisboa** or *Santos Populares*, literally the popular

○ *Established parkland sits comfortably with newer buildings*

saints' days, which include celebrations for St Anthony (12–13 June), St John (23–24 June) and St Peter (28–29 June). The streets fill with parades, music and dance, and balconies are decorated with paper lanterns, streamers and coloured lights. Locals give each other gifts of basil pots and paper carnations.

The **Sintra Music and Ballet Festival** also takes place this month and continues into July with a programme of chamber music and ballet by international performers and some of Portugal's best talent.

July

As the summer carries on heating up, **Estoril Jazz Festival** attracts plenty of top names, whilst the **Cascais Summer Festival** lights up the area with fireworks and nightly entertainment. Back in Lisbon, you can cool off at the Beer Festival in the Castelo de São Jorge with a few cold jars and then roll down to the Baixa-Chiado where the BaixAnima traditional free arts street festival takes place.

August

As well as the open-air festivals continuing through August, the Calouste Gulbenkian Foundation hosts the **Jazz em Augusto** festival in August, bringing contemporary sounds to the public. August also sees the beginning of the **Superliga** football season, so there's a chance to see either Boavista or Sporting Lisbon play.

September

The Cascais Summer Festival and the BaixAnima Street festival continue into September and bring the music-filled summer to a close, but September's events don't end there – Lisbon's second half-marathon takes place, starting at the Vasco da Gama bridge.

October
Fashion-lovers can see all the latest styles from Portuguese designers at **Moda Lisboa**. The **Gulbenkian Orchestra and Choir season** starts, and continues through to the following May.

November
Arte Lisboa, the capital's contemporary art fair, sees artists and galleries from around the world descending on the exhibition centre in the Parque das Nações.

December
Lisbon is a favourite for a **New Year's Eve** party, *Reveillon*, as stages are set up in Belém for live bands and DJs and the streets are packed with revellers.

PUBLIC HOLIDAYS
New Year's Day 1 January
Mardi Gras/Carnival February (varies)
Easter Mar/Apr (varies)
Liberty Day 25 April
Labour Day 1 May
Portugal Day 10 June
Corpus Christi 14 June
Assumption 15 August
Republic Day 5 October
All Saints' Day 1 November
Restoration (of Independence) Day 1 December
Day of Our Lady 8 December
Christmas Day 25 December

New design

It wasn't until after Portugal joined the EU in 1986 that Lisbon began to change visually. In 1988, the Centro Cultural de Belém was completed, a landmark new cultural centre with a design museum, contemporary art galleries, and meeting and conference facilities.

Despite the horrific fire in the Chiado in 1988, design looked to the future. The Museu do Chiado, stifled since its inception in 1911, was finally redesigned in 1994 (when Lisbon was European Capital of Culture). Other parts of the Chiado were rebuilt with new shopping arcades and homes, some of which were designed by Portugal's greatest contemporary architect, Alvaro Siza.

One of the biggest changes was in the east of the city, when Lisbon hosted Expo '98. Entitled 'The Oceans: A Heritage for the Future', and marking the 500th anniversary of Vasco da Gama's voyage to India, a decaying industrial area of the city was transformed into the modern and stylish Parque das Nações (see pages 110–18). Siza built the Portuguese Pavilion with its architecturally spectacular roof, whilst the rest of the park was turned into a social and cultural haven of museums, auditoriums, a conference centre, shops and restaurants, as well as the 17-km (11-mile) long Vasco da Gama Bridge.

Lisbon continues to evolve, with internationally renowned architects such as Frank Gehry, Norman Foster, Jean Nouvel and Renzo Piano. The city has found its direction once again, and, as it changes but retains its glorious past, one visit really isn't enough.

● *The state-of-the-art railway station at Parques das Nações*

History

Lisbon's turbulent past is full of invasions, occupations and war. When the Romans arrived in the 2nd century AD, they integrated the territory into the empire under the name of Felicitus Jullia, later Olissipo.

The city, now known as Lixbuna, Lizhboa and other variations, was taken by the Moors in AD 711. The Moors built houses, mosques and a fortress (on the site of the Castelo de São Jorge, see page 74) in al-Hamma (Alfama). Arabic became the official language, Islam the official religion, and the city flourished for the next four centuries.

Lisbon was made Portugal's capital in 1260, and a century later the Golden Age of Discovery was beginning. From the 14th to 16th centuries, Portugal's maritime explorers such as Bartolomeu Dias and Vasco da Gama forged routes to sail around the Cape of Good Hope and to the Americas.

Gold was discovered in Brazil, and, whilst the Portuguese royal family grew rich from its colonial pickings, life on the city's streets wasn't so glorious. In 1506, around 2,000 Jews were massacred on the streeets. Growing colonial unrest led to the Wars of Restoration, during which a group of noblemen laid siege to Lisbon in 1640. The Duke of Bragança was crowned King Dom João IV, but Spain would not recognise Portuguese independence until 1668.

It wasn't until 1755, when the Great Earthquake (and tsunami that followed) devastated the city killing 90,000 people, that ideals began to change. After what became known as the first modern disaster, the Marquês de Pombal rebuilt Lisbon (see page 58) by bringing the city centre into the Age of Enlightenment, though poor areas such as the Alfama remained medieval.

After suffering Napoleonic invasions and civil war during the 19th century, the king, Dom Manuel II, was assassinated in 1910 and the Republic born. The country remained unsettled and in 1926 a coup d'état was followed by the rise of Dr António de Oliveira Salazar to prime minister in 1932, who then led a 48-year dictatorship during which he imposed his repressive *Estado Novo*. Salazar's dictatorship ended in 1968, when serious illness finally stopped him. The 1960s had seen unrest in the colonies, gradual liberalisation of the press, and socialist cultural movements. The transition to democracy finally saw a bloodless coup, known as the Carnation Revolution. At 12.25 on 25 April 1974, the banned protest song 'Grândola, Vila Morena' was broadcast on the radio and soldiers entered the streets of Lisbon with red carnations protruding from their tanks.

Since then Portugal has pulled itself out of the past and its capital has been transformed once again. Portugal joined the EU in 1986, and Lisbon was the European Capital of Culture in 1994. The city hosted Expo '98 and, in 2004, the European Football Championships. Although the economy still struggles, these events have led to massive construction and confidence, and Lisbon is now a top city-break destination.

Lifestyle

A famous saying in Portugal is that 'Lisbon plays, Porto works and Braga prays'. Whilst people in Lisbon also work and pray, it is a vibrant capital with a laid-back café culture and lively nightlife.

This is a capital city with a busy financial district where socialising is important. Rather than hundreds of coffee shops belonging to international chains, the cafés here are individual, and there are plenty of them. There are cafés where people spend an hour chatting to friends and sipping *um galão* (milky coffee in a glass), and others where they stand at the counter for a quick snack *pastel de nata* (Portuguese custard tart), but there are also internet cafés and coffee kiosks in the street.

Although there are sandwich bars in Lisbon, people can take two hours for lunch and eat properly, so you'll often find that the shops and some museums close at this time, too. Portions tend to be large, but don't be afraid of leaving a little on your plate – they'll take it as a compliment that they've fed you enough! In some places you can order a main course to share between two people.

Generally the Portuguese are very polite, so unless you're very familiar, you should say *bom dia* (good morning) or *boa tarde* (good afternoon) rather than *olá*. You're unlikely to see anyone taking their shoes off in a public place, except on the beach, as it's considered bad manners, so it's best to make sure you have comfortable footwear and don't flip them off in the middle of a restaurant or park.

The Portuguese do like a drink and, in fact, have a really high national average of alcohol consumption. However, you're unlikely to see drunken Portuguese falling out of the bars as in some other countries. Even though locals tend to go out late at night, even the younger people can spend hours pondering over one drink before heading on to a club after midnight. It's all about taking your time and enjoying the food, wine, good company and surroundings more than the actual alcohol content. There's no rush, just enjoy yourself!

⬤ *Stop and relax at a café in Parque Eduardo VII*

Culture

Fado remains at the forefront of Lisbon's musical identity. Whether you love or hate the melancholic sounds of fado music, it attracts thousands of tourists and locals to the restaurants and bars of the Bairro Alto and Alfama every year.

There are two forms of fado: one developed among the privileged students of the University of Coimbra, whilst the other developed among the working classes in Lisbon. Here it was sung by social outcasts, and also linked to the seafarers during the Golden Age of Discovery (*fado do marinhero*), when sailors yearned for their homeland.

Fado is sung by a solo vocalist and usually accompanied by a *viola* (Spanish guitar) and a *guitarra* (pear-shaped, 12-string Portuguese guitar). Lisbon's most famous fadista is Amália Rodrigues, who rose to fame in the 1950s and 1960s, but others have followed in her wake. (See pages 67–71 for ideas on where to hear fado.)

Lisbon is home to the Orquestra and Coro Gulbenkian (see opposite), has a thriving jazz scene, popular music venues, such as the Pavilhão Atlânticok, and several music festivals. However, there is plenty of dance in the city, from the Companhia Nacional do Bailado to visiting contemporary dance groups.

The Baixa, Chiado and Bairro Alto were favourite haunts of artists and writers, and today you'll find monuments to Luís de Camões and Fernando Pessoa in these places (see pages 58–71). Outside A Brasileira café in the Bairro Alto is a seated statue of Pessoa; he used to frequent the café and today it is still popular with arty types who meet there every morning for a chat.

HIGHLIGHTS IN THE VISUAL AND PERFORMING ARTS INCLUDE:

- **The Calouste Gulbenkian Foundation** (see pages 89–91), the premier arts organisation in Portugal, home to the Orquestra Gulbenkian and Coro Gulbenkian, as well as the Museu Gulbenkian and Centro de Arte Moderna.
- **Centro Cultural de Belém** (see pages 101–2). The largest and one of the most popular contemporary arts venues in the city, the CCB houses the Museu do Design, hosts regular exhibitions by international artists in its galleries, and opera, ballet, classical music and jazz in its Performance Centre.
- The **Museu Nacional de Arte Antiga** (see page 103) is considered one of the most important museums in the country. Located in a 17th-century palace, the highlight is its collection of 15th- to 19th-century Portuguese and European paintings.
- **Museu do Chiado** (see pages 64–5) was Lisbon's first modern art gallery and has an impressive collection of works by Portugal's most representative 20th-century artists.
- **Teatro Camões** (see page 114) is the city's newest theatre, in the Parque das Nações, and home to the Companhia Nacional do Bailado, the country's national ballet company.
- **Teatro Nacional de São Carlos** (see page 65). This theatre replaced the pre-1755 building that stood here and has a fabulous rococo interior.

Mother and child statue in Parque Eduardo VII

Check out a performance at the National Theatre

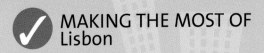

Shopping

WHERE TO SHOP

Lisbon has boutiques, markets and traditional street shopping, as well as large shopping centres. In the Baixa-Chiado area, particularly along the Rua Augusta, there's a mix of international chain stores, as well as small traditional shops selling leather goods and jewellery. Indulge your penchant for designer labels on the Avenida da Liberdade or opt for the traditional shopping area on the Campo de Ourique. There's a branch of the Spanish department store El Corte Inglés in Alto del Parque Eduardo VII. Amoreiras and Colombo are large shopping centres, but the newest is Vasco da Gama in Parque das Nações, which has 164 shops on four floors.

MARKETS

The Feira da Ladra is a flea market in the Alfama. If you like to rummage for a bargain among gems and junk, this market is open every Tuesday and Saturday. There's also a fish market in Cais do Sodré, selling everything from the wet pulp of octopus to *bacalhau* (dried codfish).

WHAT TO BUY

There's a good choice of leather goods, lace and linen. Look out for copper dishes, painted terracotta ceramics and *azulejos* tiles. From

SHOPPING CARD
This card lasts for either 24 or 72 hours and can be purchased from the tourist office (Lisbon Welcome Centre). It gives up to 20 per cent off in more than 175 shops in the Baixa, Chiado and Avenida da Liberdade.

the supermarket you can pick up a selection of *presunto* (smoked ham), *chouriço* (spicy sausage), wines from Estremadura, Beiras, Dão and the Douro, port wine from the Douro and *vinho verde* (green wine) from the Minho.

🔺 *Souvenirs rule the roost here ...*

USEFUL SHOPPING PHRASES

What time do the shops open/close?
A que horas abrem/fecham as lojas?
A kee orah abrayng/fayshown ash lohzhash?

How much is this?
Quanto custa isto?
Kwantoo kooshta eeshtoo?

Can I try this on?
Posso provar este?
Possoo proovahr aysht?

My size is ...
O meu tamanho (número) é ...
Oo mayo tamanyo (noomiroo) eh ...

I'll take this one, thank you
Levo este, obrigado
Lehvoo aysht, ohbreegahdoo

This is too large/too small/too expensive.
Do you have any others?
Este é muito grande/muito pequeno/muito caro. Tem outros?
Aysht eh muingtoo grangdi/muingtoo pikaynoo/muingtoo kahroo. Tayng ohtroosh?

Eating & drinking

Eating in Lisbon is a real pleasure, as the Portuguese love their food, menus are full of variety, and portions are generous.

Traditional Portuguese restaurants compete with a large number of international eateries. Try one of the Brazilian restaurants, which often have buffet menus that include cold meats and fish, as well as hot meat from the spit. There are plenty of pizzerias, steak houses, Chinese and even a few Indian restaurants, as well as the usual choice of fast food and sandwiches. Vegetarians sometimes find it easier to eat in the international restaurants, as the local diet doesn't regularly include options for non-meat eaters.

Lisbon's proximity to the sea means that fish and seafood feature high on the menu, but there are plenty of meat dishes, too. Soup is the mainstay of the Portuguese diet and you'll find it on many menus as a starter, particularly *caldo verde* (a delicious cabbage soup made from chicken stock and a slice of *chouriço* (spicy sausage) and *sopa de legumes* (vegetable soup).

Bacalhau is another common dish and you'll often see it hanging up in the shops. The most popular salt codfish recipe is *bacalhau com natas,* salt codfish with cream and potatoes. Squid (*lulas*) is another common option and often fried in batter – the larger ones in rings and the baby squid fried whole, which are delicious as the legs go all crispy. Also look out for *camarão* (prawns), *gambas grelhadas* (grilled king prawns), *caldeirada* (fish stew), *lulas*

RESTAURANT CARD
The Lisboa Restaurant Card is valid for 72 hours and can be purchased from the tourist office (Lisbon Welcome Centre). It offers discounts in around 40 quality Lisbon restaurants.

recheadas (stuffed squid), *polvo grelhado* (grilled octopus), *sardinhas assadas* (grilled sardines), *robalo* (sea bass) and *sargo* (sea bream). These will often be served with potatoes (*batatas*), chips (*batatas fritas*), mixed salad (*salada mixta*) with olives (*azeitonas*) or vegetables such as spinach (*espinafres*).

Meat also features high on the menu and includes *bife tornedo* (succulent, quite rare piece of beef), *bifes de Perú* (turkey steak), *cabrito assado* (grilled kid), *costeleta de vitela* (veal cutlets/chops), *frango no churrasco* (barbecued chicken), *leitão assado* (spit-roast suckling pig) and *lombo de porco assado* (roast pork).

Many of the desserts and cakes are made with eggs, including *pasteis de nata* or *pasteis de Belém* (custard tart), *papos de anjo* (egg-based pastry dish) and *pudim* (crème caramel).

◯ *Traditional* bacalhau *is widely available and delicious*

Cafés are your best option for less formal dining; try one of the *cervejarias* (café/bar) for snacks, such as toasted cheese and ham sandwiches (*tosta mixta*) or surf 'n' turf of steak with crab claws (they'll give you a hammer to crack them) and beer or coffee. Some restaurants will automatically put a basket of bread and cheeses in front of you, but unless you want to eat and pay for these, you should ask them to take them away.

There are many ways to drink coffee: *uma bica* (small coffee, like an espresso), *um meia de leite* (coffee with milk), *um garoto* (small coffee with milk) and *um galão* (milky coffee in a tall glass). You can also buy tea (*chá*) but you'll have to ask for milk (*leite*). There are plenty of regional wines in Portugal, including the Estremadura region (around Lisbon), Beiras, Dão, Douro (where port wine comes from) and the Minho (where *vinho verde* is produced).

⬤ *You're never far from a good coffee shop in Chiado*

USEFUL DINING PHRASES

I would like a table for ... people
Queria uma mesa para ... pessoas
Kireea ooma mehza para ... pesoash

May I have the bill, please?	**Waiter/waitress!**
Pode-me dar a conta, por favor?	Faz favor!
Pohd-mi dahr er kohngta, poor favohr?	*Fash favohr!*

Could I have it well-cooked/medium/rare, please?
Posso escolher bem passado/médio/mal passado, por favor?
Possoo ishkoolyer bayng pasahdoo/mahl pasahdoo, poor favohr?

I am a vegetarian. Does this contain meat?
Sou vegetariano. Isto tem carne?
Soh vezhetahreeahnoo. Ishtoo tehng kahrni?

Where is the toilet (restroom) please?
Por favor, onde são os lavabos?
Poor favohr, ohngdee sowng oos lavahboosh?

I would like a cup of/two cups of/another coffee/tea
Queria uma chávena de/duas chávenas de/outro café/chá
Kireea ooma shahvna di/dooash shahvnash di ohtroo kafeh/shah

Entertainment & nightlife

There's no shortage of entertainment in Lisbon, but don't expect the Portuguese to be falling out of the pubs. They know how to have fun, but generally stay well in control. Part of the reason is that they eat well and drink slowly. Dinner can be around 20.00 or 21.00 and accompanied by music in a fado bar, or you can enjoy a drink before heading out to a club.

BARS & CLUBS

Clubs don't generally get going until midnight. Traditionally the Bairro Alto was the place to go out drinking and clubbing, and there still isn't a shortage of places to eat, drink and dance. There is a concentration of bars along Rua de Diário de Noticias and adjacent streets. The Alfama is less of a clubbing area, with the exception of the city's most famous club, the Lux Bar by Santa Apolonia Station.

Two areas have really transformed nightlife in Lisbon: the Parque das Nações and Alcântara. The first has a long line of riverfront restaurant-bars, some of which become clubs later in the evening. Alcântara and the former Docas (docks) by 25 de Abril bridge include some of the city's trendiest restaurants, bars and nightclubs.

MUSIC

Lisbon has a good choice of music from fado clubs where you can eat and drink, jazz clubs such as the Hot Clube, Speakeasy and Blues Bar, as well as larger venues, such as the Coliseu dos Recreios and Pavilhão Atlântico, where international bands play. There are also open-air events throughout the year from New Year's Eve, when

● *A beer house in Chiado*

there are stages and live bands in Belém, to the Superbock
Superrock festival in Parque das Nações, which includes a line-up
of internationally renowned groups. The tourist office publishes
Follow Me, a monthly magazine in English that highlights
forthcoming live events and festivals.

Tickets for live events can be bought from FNAC bookshops
(in most shopping centres, as well as the Baixa-Chiado), or online
at Ⓦ www.fnac.pt or Ⓦ http://ticketline.sapo.pt

🔺 *A souk bar in the Bairro Alto*

Coliseu dos Recreios (see page 89) is a popular venue for both popular music and classical concerts.

Fado houses with live entertainment daily are dotted around the **Bairro Alto** (see pages 67–71) and the **Alfama** (see pages 82–3), and retain their popularity both with locals and tourists.

Hot Clube de Portugal (see page 95) is a legendary jazz club that still retains its status despite the arrival of trendy **Speakeasy** (see page 108) and **Blues Café** (see page 107)

Pavilhão Atlântico (see page 114) is the biggest venue for popular music and sports events.

THEATRE, OPERA & PERFORMING ARTS

Theatre might not be the best live entertainment unless your Portuguese is particularly good. However, most of the large theatres in Lisbon also have a decent programme of classical concerts, opera and ballet.

Teatro Camões (see page 114) is the city's newest theatre, in the Parque das Nações, and home to the Companhia Nacional do Bailado, the country's national ballet company.

Teatro Nacional Dona Maria II (see page 65), historically one of the city's most important theatres, now presents a programme of theatre, circus and performance art.

Teatro Nacional de São Carlos (see page 65) replaced the pre-1755 building that stood here and has a fabulous rococo interior. It has a busy programme of opera, classical music and theatre.

CINEMA

There are multiplex cinemas in the large shopping centres. Most films are shown in their original language with subtitles. Londres cinema (Avenida da Roma 7A) shows art-house films.

Sport & relaxation

SPECTATOR SPORTS
Football
The Portuguese love football, whether it's an international match, a Superliga team or a local club. There are two Superliga teams in Lisbon: Benfica and Sporting Lisbon. Benfica is based at the new Estádio da Luz (ⓦ www.slbenfica.pt) that hosted the final of Euro 2004. Sporting Lisbon (ⓦ www.sporting.pt) is based at the Estádio José de Alvalade. Whilst it can be difficult to get tickets for the larger matches, you might be able to buy a ticket on the day of the match from the stadium. See ⓦ www.fpf.pt

Racing
The Estoril Race Track is a Formula One circuit and hosts car and motorbike racing throughout most of the year. They also organise days when you can race your own bike around the track. ⓦ www.circuito-estoril.pt

PARTICIPATORY SPORTS
Golf
Estoril has quite a concentration of top-notch golf courses, including the Estoril Golf Course (ⓞ 21 468 0054), Penha Longa (ⓞ 21 924 9031), Quinta da Marinha (ⓞ 21 486 0180) and Oitavos Golf (ⓞ 21 486 0600).

Surfing & watersports
There are sailing and watersports schools dotted all along the beach from Cascais Marina to Oeiras, as well as the Sintra coast further north. The most popular sport among the younger crowd is surfing,

and **Carcavelos** is one of the best places, along with **Guincho** and **Colares**. You can hire equipment and have lessons with Super Winds in Oeiras (ⓣ 21 469 4602), Surfing Clube de Portugal in São Pedro de Estoril (ⓣ 21 466 4516) and Windsurf Café in Carcavelos (ⓣ 21 457 8965), or catch a few waves on your own board. Most of these schools offer windsurfing and body boarding, too.

Horse riding

There are several places to go horse riding, including the Quinta da Marinha resort (ⓣ 21 486 9433) and the Manuel Passolo school in the Parque Municipal de Gandarinha (ⓣ 21 482 1720).

Tennis

Tennis can be played at the Quinta da Marinha resort (ⓣ 21 486 0180) and the Clube de Ténis de Estoril (ⓣ 21 466 2770) on Avenida Conde de Barcelona, which has 18 floodlit courts and often hosts international matches.

● *The Pavilhão Atlântico is a major sporting venue*

Accommodation

Lisbon has a diverse range of accommodation to suit all budgets and tastes, from luxury 5-star hotels with pools to mid-priced 3-star hotels and *residenciais* (bed and breakfast).

There is plenty of accommodation available around the Bairro Alto and Chiado, including some of the trendiest (and most expensive) hotels, alongside budget options. This area is ideal if you're after a party weekend, as it won't be far back from your hotel from either the Bairro Alto or the Docas.

The hotels in the streets around Parque Eduardo VII and Amoreiras are favoured for business trips, but don't let this put you off if you want to be in a quieter part of town.

Parque das Nações is also popular for business with its easy access to the airport and the Feira International de Lisboa (FIL), the city's conference centre. It is also good for children, as there are several attractions for kids here, and you are close to shopping, eating and drinking venues. However, if you are with children or are looking for some surf, you might prefer to stay out of Lisbon in Cascais or Estoril (see pages 130–1), with easier access to the beach. Here you'll find everything from camping and small hotels to resort hotels and apartment hotels.

For romantic weekends, there are manor houses, historic and boutique hotels in Sintra (see pages 141–2), Chiado and Alfama. Portugal's *pousadas* (luxury, historic hotels), often in converted

PRICE RATINGS
The price symbols indicate the approximate price of a double room for two people, including breakfast:
£ up to £50; ££ £50–£120; £££ over £120

historic buildings, are also popular, but the nearest ones to Lisbon are in Queluz, towards Sintra (see pages 141–2), and just outside Setúbal, so this is a better option if you are staying longer and want to go exploring. Also look out for *estalagems*, state-run hotels.

You can easily book hotels online at a number of websites, many of which offer reasonable discounts. As well as www.expedia.com and www.hotels.com, try www.maisturismo.com for a range of accommodation; www.pousadas.pt and www.heritage.pt for historic hotels; www.solaresdeportugal.pt for manor houses; and www.portugalvirtual.pt for *residenciais*. It can be cheaper to book directly. If you find yourself without accommodation, contact the tourist office, or head to the Bairro Alto or Chiado area and try one of the *residenciais*.

HOTELS & GUESTHOUSES
Hotel Nacional £ A comfortable hotel within easy reach of the Praça do Marquês de Pombal, with private bathrooms, buffet breakfast room and a bar.
ⓐ Rua Castilho 34 ⓣ 21 355 4433 ⓦ www.hotel-nacional.com

◯ *View from the top of the Four Seasons Hotel*

Residencial Dom Sancho I £ Conveniently located for the Bairro Alto and Alfama, this is a family-run hotel. Rooms have private bathrooms, there's a breakfast room decorated with *azulejos*, and room service.

ⓐ Avenida da Liberdade 202–203 ⓣ 21 354 8648
ⓦ www.portugalvirtual.pt

◑ *Le Meridien Hotel, viewed from Parque Eduardo VII*

Residencial Florescente £ This friendly hotel is located just off Praça dos Restauradores, close to the Baixa and Bairro Alto, as well as the metro station. There are various-sized rooms, all with en-suite bathrooms.
ⓐ Rua das Portas de Santo Antão 99, 3rd and 4th floors
ⓣ 21 342 6609 Ⓦ www.portugalvirtual.pt

Hotel Açores Lisboa ££ A contemporary hotel in the financial district, five minutes from the Praça do Marquês de Pombal and right by the metro station at Praça de Espanha. Facilities include a restaurant, bar, terrace, TV lounge, business centre and private indoor car park.
ⓐ Avenida columbano Bordalo Pinheiro 1 ⓣ 21 722 2920
ⓔ reservas@bensaude.pt

Hotel Britânia ££ Designed by famous Portuguese modernist architect Casiano Branco in the 1940s, its art deco ambience has been renovated. Ideally located in a quiet street just off the Avenida da Liberdade.
ⓐ Rus Rodrigues Sampaio 17 ⓣ 21 315 5016
Ⓦ www.heritage.pt ⓔ britania.hotel@heritage.pt

Hotel Dom Pedro Lisboa ££ Located opposite the Amoreiras shopping centre, this tall hotel in mirrored blue glass is close to the business centre. A modern 5-star hotel, there are stunning views across the city.
ⓐ Avenida Eng Duarte Pacheco 24 ⓣ 21 389 6600
Ⓦ www.dompedro.com ⓔ dp.lisboa@dompedro.com

Hotel Miraparque ££ This hotel overlooks the Parque Eduardo VII and has a quiet location. It also has its own restaurant and bar.
ⓐ Avenida Sidónio Pais 12 ☎ 21 352 4286 ⓦ www.miraparque.com
ⓔ hotel@miraparque.com

Hotel Tivoli Tejo ££ A modern hotel in the Parque das Nações, opposite the Vasco da Gama shopping centre and 10 minutes from the airport. There's a heated indoor pool, health club, bar and two restaurants.
ⓐ Avenida Dom João II ☎ 21 891 5100 ⓦ www.tivolihotels.com
ⓔ httejo@tivolihotels.com

As Janelas Verdes £££ Once the home of Portuguese writer Eça de Queiroz, this former 18th-century mansion still has a library on the top floor. It has pretty gardens and is located near the river by the Museu Nacional de Arte Antiga.
ⓐ Rua das Janelas Verdes 47 ☎ 21 396 8143 ⓦ www.heritage.pt
ⓔ jverdes@heritage.pt

Bairro Alto Hotel £££ A new 'boutique' hotel in the heart of the old city, it has easy access to cultural attractions as well as shopping and nightlife. All of its 55 rooms are kitted out in the latest technology, and there's also a restaurant, café and fitness room.
ⓐ Praça Luis de Camões ☎ 21 340 8222 ⓦ www.hotelbairroalto.com

Hotel Avenida Palace £££ The first palace hotel in the city, it is located by Praça dos Restauradores and is convenient to the Baixa, Bairro Alto and Avenida da Liberdade.
ⓐ Rua 1 de Dezembro 123 ☎ 21 321 8100 ⓦ www.hotel-avenida-palace.pt ⓔ reservas@hotel-avenida-palace.pt

Hotel da Torre £££ Located near the Mosteiro dos Jerónimos and Torre de Belém, the hotel is decorated with 19th-century tiles and has a restaurant and bar.
ⓐ Rua dos Jerónimos 8 ⓣ 21 361 9940
ⓦ www.maisturismo.pt/torre.htm
ⓔ hoteldatorre.belem@mail.telepac.pt

Lapa Palace £££ A former aristocrat's palace built in 1870, this luxury hotel is set on a hill amid tropical gardens with spectacular views of the river and city. There are outdoor and indoor heated pools and a spa.
ⓐ Rua Pau de Bandeira 4 ⓣ 21 395 0665 ⓦ www.lapa-palace.com
ⓔ info@lapa-palace.com

Palácio Belmonte £££ A 14th-century palace, this romantic hotel is located in the Alfama by the Castelo de São Jorge. The refurbishment has maintained the ancient beams and 18th-century tiles. Each suite has been individually designed and named after a Portuguese personality.
ⓐ Páteo Dom Fradique 14 ⓣ 21 881 6600
ⓦ www.palaciobelmonte.com ⓔ office@palaciobelmonte.com

Solar do Castelo £££ This is a historic hotel, located within the walls of the Castelo de São Jorge. Known as the Kitchen's Mansion, it was constructed where the kitchens of the former Alcaçova Palace once stood.
ⓐ Rua das Cozinhas 2 ⓣ 21 887 0907 ⓦ www.heritage.pt
ⓔ solar.castelo@heritage.pt

THE BEST OF LISBON

You could easily fill a week with Lisbon's interesting sights, but if you just have a short time, here is the pick of the crop.

TOP 10 ATTRACTIONS

- **Castelo de São Jorge** Testament to the city's history, see the castle's dry moat, towers, look-outs and squares (see page 74)

- **Tram No. 28 ride** A quick and easy way to see the Bairro Alto, Baixa and Alfama without a tour guide (see page 42)

- **The Alfama district** A tangle of narrow streets; see the cathedral, castle, Jewish quarter, museums and great city views (see pages 72–83)

- **Torre de Belém** Superb example of *manuelino* architecture; look out for the stone ropes, heraldic motifs and carved rhinoceros (see page 101)

- **Mosteiro dos Jerónimos** Architectural masterpiece (see page 98)

- **Fundação Calouste Gulbenkian** Modern art, lush gardens and musical history in the making (see pages 89–91)

- **Elevador de Santa Justa** Ride the elevator for great views over the Baixa (see page 60)

- **Museu Nacional de Arte Antiga** 17th-century palace (see page 103)

- **Baixa District** Shopaholics' paradise (see pages 58–71)

- **Museu Nacional do Azulejo** 16th-century former convent with superb collection of *azulejos* (see page 79)

○ *Alfama is bursting with exciting vistas*

Here's a quick guide to the best of Lisbon, depending on the time you have available.

HALF-DAY: LISBON IN A HURRY

Jump on the vintage tram No. 28, which clatters along the narrow streets through several key districts. There are stops (*paragems*) along the route in Campo Ourique, Estrela, Bairro Alto, Baixa, Alfama and Martim Moniz. Hop off at Alfama and visit Castelo de São Jorge with its spectacular city views. If you have time, stop for a coffee in the Largo das Portas do Sol before heading back.

1 DAY: TIME TO SEE A LITTLE MORE

Again, take tram No. 28 up to the Alfama and visit the Castelo de São Jorge, but stop for lunch in or around the castle. Wind your way back downhill past the Jewish quarter and the Casa dos Bicos, then head along to the Baixa for some shopping. If your feet are tired from Lisbon's hills, take the Elevador de Glória from Praça dos Restauradores up to the Bairro Alto and walk round to the Solar do Vinho do Porto where you can sink into armchairs with a well-earned glass of port.

2–3 DAYS: SHORT CITY BREAK

Explore several distinct areas of the city. Don't miss out on the Alfama, Castelo de São Jorge and shopping in the Baixa. Spend some time soaking up the atmosphere of the Bairro Alto and Chiado, visiting the Convento do Carmo and Museu do Chiado and make time for its cafés and a very Portuguese evening of fado, before heading off to a club in the renovated Docas. A whole day is needed to take in the sights of Belém, with the Mosteiro dos Jerónimos and Torre de Belém at the top of the list, but don't miss the Centro

Cultural de Belém, the Discoveries Monument and the cakes at the famous Pastéis de Belém. Another day could easily be spent in the Parque das Nações with its superb Oceanário (Oceanarium), Teleférico (cable car) and the huge Vasco da Gama shopping centre, as well as plenty of riverside restaurants and bars.

LONGER: ENJOYING LISBON TO THE FULL

Visit the Fundação Calouste Gulbenkian, find a retreat in one of the city parks, such as the lush Jardim Botánico and Parque Eduardo VII, or take a boat trip on the Tagus River. Make time for a trip to Sintra to see the Castelo dos Mouros, palaces and museums, and other excursion towns such as Fátima and Evora. Or head to Cascais and Estoril for beaches, watersports, golf, a young crowd and plenty of vibrant nightlife.

● *The city's gardens are blissfully beautiful*

Something for nothing

Exploring Lisbon on foot is a tiring but worthwhile experience. As it is built on seven hills, Castelo, Estrela, Graça, Monte, Penha de França, Santa Catarina and São Pedro de Alcântara, you can gain a

● *There are priceless views from the city's* miradouros

vista of the city at no cost. At various points around the city, *miradouros* (belvederes or viewing points) have been built to enhance the view and let you relax as you take in the sights.

After climbing the steep Alfama streets to the Castelo de São Jorge, you'll be rewarded with fabulous views in the first castle square across the Baixa and Chiado. Look out for the ruins of the Convento do Carmo, the domes of Santa Engrácia and Basilica de Estrela as well as the Parque Eduardo VII and the River Tagus. Just a walk downhill from the castle, you'll find two adjacent viewing points, Portas da Sol and Santa Luzia, from where you can peer over the rooftops of the Alfama to the river. At Santa Luzia, look for the old *azulejos* tiles to see an image of Lisbon prior to the 1755 earthquake.

On the other side of the hill, in Graça, is another viewing point in Largo da Graça with similar views as the castle, but it's much more romantic here and you can look up towards the castle, relax in the shade of the pine trees and gaze over the rooftops of the Mouraria.

Walk to the top of the slanting Parque Eduardo VII to have a well-defined view of the park's formal gardens and straight down the Avenida da Liberdade.

From the *miradouro* at São Pedro de Alcântara, in the Bairro Alto, there's a panoramic view of the castle, plus the Baixa and Avenida da Liberdade. For a view in the opposite direction, head to Santa Catarina at the other end of the Bairro Alto, from where you can see the Basilica da Estrela, the districts of Lapa and Madragoa and over the roofs to the port.

The other viewing points around the city, notably the top of the Discoveries Monument, the Torre de Belém, the Vasco da Gama Tower, Elevador de Santa Justa and the Christ the Redeemer statue, are not free.

When it rains

There are so many museums, cultural and historic sites and other attractions in Lisbon that you won't be short of things to do if it rains. Although the weather is generally fair, it does rain from time to time and you don't want to be caught slipping down the cobbled streets through Alfama or heading for the beach in Cascais. With the help of the efficient metro system and trams, you can zip across the city from one attraction to the next.

The Museu Gulbenkian and the Centro de Arte Moderna (see pages 89–91) are a good place to start. You could easily spend a day looking round them both – and there's a restaurant to stop for lunch. Then if it stops raining you can head straight outdoors to the lush Gulbenkian gardens or walk back to town through the Parque Eduardo VII.

If you're caught in a shower in the Bairro Alto, head downhill to see the Museu do Chiado's modern art collection or immerse yourself in a long lunch at one of the numerous restaurants there.

You could spend a few hours in the Museu Nacional de Arte Antiga, where the collection of Portuguese painting will keep you intrigued. Also the Docas are not far away if you want to spend a few hours undercover eating and drinking until the rain stops.

Another option is Belém. You can hop from the Mosteiro dos Jerónimos next door to the Museu Nacional da Aqueologia and the Museu da Marinha, or nip over the road to the Centro Cultural de Belém with its contemporary exhibitions, Museu de Design and restaurant.

Or spend the day indulging yourself in one of the shopping centres, which generally open from 10.00 until midnight – there are metro stations at Colombo and Vasco da Gama (Oriente) shopping centres. You can stay for lunch here too, and this doesn't necessarily mean settling for fast food – there are quality restaurants alongside sandwiches, snacks and coffee bars.

If you opt for Parque das Nações, you could see the wonders of the underwater world at Oceanário and discover something scientific at the Pavilhão de Conhecimento, a particularly good option if you're with children.

🔺 *The Vasco da Gama shopping centre is a great place to spend a rainy day*

On arrival

TIME DIFFERENCES

Portugal follows Greenwich Mean Time (GMT). During Daylight
Saving Time (late Mar–late Sept), the clocks are put forward by one
hour. In the Portuguese summer, at 12.00, the time in Australia,
New Zealand, South Africa, UK and USA is as follows:

Australia: Eastern Standard Time 21.00, Central Standard Time 20.30,
Western Standard Time 19.00
New Zealand: 23.00
South Africa: 13.00
UK: 12.00
USA: Eastern Time 07.00; Central Time 06.00; Mountain Time 05.00;
Pacific Time 04.00; Alaska 03.00

ARRIVING
By air

Aeroporto de Portela, Lisbon's international airport, is located in the
north of the city and is the busiest and most important airport in
the country. You will find Tourist Information in the Arrivals Terminal.
If you want to take a taxi into the city centre, you should buy a
voucher here. However, the quick and efficient AEROBUS runs every
20 minutes from the airport to Cais do Sodré via Saldanha, Marquês
Pombal, Avenida da Liberdade, Restauradores, Rossio and Praça do
Comércio. Tickets can be purchased onboard and cost €1.20 for a
single. There are also a few local buses, including No. 44, which goes
to Parque das Nações, and an hourly Airport Shuttle Bus to
Cascais/Estoril (€8.50).
Portuguese airports Ⓦ www.ana-aeroportos.pt

By rail

Portugal's Alfa-Pendular trains are the best ones to take if travelling long distances. Clean, fast and reasonably priced, these run to Faro in the south and Coimbra, Porto and Braga in the north, with a few stops in between. Long-distance trains leave from Oriente and Santa Apolonia stations, whilst trains to Cascais/Estoril leave from Cais do Sodré, and to Sintra from Entrecampos.

Portuguese trains ⓦ www.cp.pt

By bus

There is no central coach station but the main stopping point is on Avenida Casal Ribeiro, just north of the city centre. There is a comprehensive city bus service in Lisbon and night buses run from Cais do Sodré through the main areas of the city. Tickets can be bought from the driver but it's cheaper to buy multiples or passes for a day or longer.

Red Expressos ⓦ www.rede-expressos.pt

By ferry

Small ferries (*cacilheiros*) are used often here by locals travelling to and from work on the south side of the Tagus. The main ferry route is from Terreiro do Paço across the river, but tourist boats also operate between here and Parque das Nações.

Transejo ⓦ www.transtejo.pt

FINDING YOUR FEET

You'll need a map to find your way through some areas of the city, but don't panic if you do feel lost as it will not be long before you will find a viewing point and be able to reorientate yourself. Lisbon's *bairros* have distinct characteristics.

Ponte Vasco da Gama

Lumiar Ⓜ

Quinta das
Conchas

✚

Aeroporto de
Portela ✈

AVENIDA CIDADE DO PORTO

AVENIDA DOUTOR ALFREDO BENSAÚDE

AVENIDA DE BERLIM

INFANTE DOM HENRIQUE

**Torre Vasco
da Gama**

**Parque
das Nações**

Estação
do Oriente 🚊
Ⓜ Oriente

**Pavilhão
Atlântico**

Oceanário

*Doca dos
Olivais*

Campo
Grande

Ⓜ AVENIDA MARECHAL CRAVEIRO LOPES

CAMPO GRANDE

AVENIDA DO BRASIL

ALMIRANTE

AVENIDA MARECHAL GOMES DA COSTA

Olivais

Ⓜ Cabo
Ruivo

Alvalade

✚

Estádio
Primeiro
de Maio

Ⓜ Entre
Campos

Roma

*Parque da
Bela Vista*

AVENIDA DOS ESTADOS UNIDOS DA AMÉRICA

Chelas

SANTO

RUA CINTURA DO PORTO

INFANTE DOM HENRIQUE

✚

Ⓜ Campo Pequeno

Areeiro

**CAMPO
PEQUENO**

AVENIDA JOÃO XXI

ALMIRANTE REIS

MANUEL

Bela
Vista

Olaias

AVENIDA

SALDANHA

Alameda

Picoas

Ⓜ Saldanha

RUA MORAIS SOARES

AVENIDA DA REPÚBLICA

AVENIDA FONTES

Ⓜ Parque

**Marquês
de Pombal**

Ⓜ ✚ 🚓

Ⓜ Marquês
de Pombal

Arroios

Anjos

✚

Ⓜ Avenida

*Jardim
Botânico*

Intendente

GRAÇA

AVENIDA INFANTE DOM HENRIQUE

**Coliseu dos
Recreios**

Ⓜ Restauradores

Martim Moniz

MOURARIA

Estação
Santa Apolónia

ℹ

**Teatro Nacional
Dona Maria II**

**Castelo de
São Jorge**

Rossio Ⓜ

Ⓜ Santa
Apolónia

BAIXA

Ⓜ Baixa-
Chiado

ALFAMA

Casa do Fado

CHIADO

Casa dos Bicos

Cais do
Sodré

ℹ PRAÇA
DO
COMÉRCIO

✝ **Sé Catedral**

*Doca do
Jardim do
Tabaco*

*Cais das
Colunas*

*Doca da
Marinha*

N

Ⓜ	Metro Stop
✝	Cathedral
🚌	Coach Stn
🚓	Police Stn
ℹ	Information
✈	Airport
🚊	Railway Stn
✚	Hospital

Lisbon

0 _____ 500 metres

0 _____ 500 yards

Whilst Portugal's crime rate is lower than some countries, tourists are often targeted by opportunists, and there has been a rise in the number of pickpockets in the past decade, particularly on tram No. 28. Also avoid walking home through dark streets such as the Alfama and Bairro Alto late at night. You can always ask for a taxi from a bar or restaurant to your hotel.

ORIENTATION

Lisbon lies on the north/east bank of the mouth of the River Tagus and is built on seven hills: Castelo, Estrela, Graça, Monte, Penha de França, São Pedro de Alcântara and Santa Catarina. It's better known

IF YOU GET LOST, TRY ...

Excuse me, do you speak English?
Desculpe, fala Inglês?
Dishkoolp, fahla eenglays?

Excuse me, is this the right way to ... the cathedral/the tourist office/the castle/the old town?
Desculpe é este o caminho certo para ... a catedral/os serviços de informações turísticas (o turismo)/o castelo/a cidade velha?
Dishkoolp, eh aysht oo kameenyo sehrtoo para ... er katidrahl/oos sirveessoos de eemfoormasoyesh tooreehshteekash (oo tooreesmoo)/oo kastehloo/er seedahd vehlya?

Can you point to it on my map?
Pode indicá-lo no meu mapa?
Pohd eendeecahloo noo mayo mahpa?

by its *bairros* (neighbourhoods). The easiest place to start is the Baixa, easily navigable because of its grid-like structure from the Praça do Comércio on the riverside north of Rossio Square.

To the east of the Baixa is the Alfama, recognisable by its tangle of streets and crowned by the Castelo de São Jorge. Beyond Alfama is the traditional neighbourhood of Graça, which boasts fabulous views of the city, and next door is Santa Apolonia on the riverside and the location of one of the major train stations. Further northeast lie the Parque das Nações and the Vasco da Gama bridge.

North of the Baixa and Rossio Square, the Avenida da Liberdade leads up to Praça Marquês de Pombal, a large roundabout with the Parque Eduardo VII to the north. The main business areas of the city are located west and north of Pombal.

To the west of the Baixa are the lively old artistic districts of the Chiado and the Bairro Alto, and beyond to Estrela and Madragoa. West along the river is the renovated dock area of Alcântara and the 25 de Abril bridge, from where you can see the towering Cristo Rei (Christ the Redeemer) statue (although it is a miniature of the one in Rio de Janeiro). Westwards from the bridge is Belém and the coast road out of Lisbon to Cascais and Estoril.

GETTING AROUND

You will probably need to use the city's public transport system at some point, as Lisbon is both hilly and spread out. Buses are run by Carris and trams are also a good option, depending on where you are going, as are the funiculars. The old tram No. 28 is a good way of ascending to Castelo São Jorge in Alfama, and also travels between Ourique and Graça via Estrela, Bairro Alto and Baixa. Modern tram No. 15 is the best way of getting to Belém from the old city and leaves from Praça do Comércio.

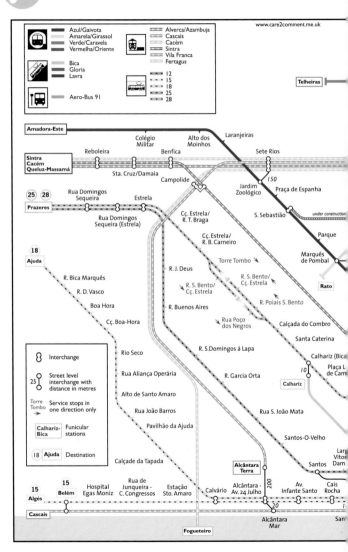

www.care2comment.me.uk

Legend:
- Azul/Gaivota
- Amarela/Girassol
- Verde/Caravela
- Vermelha/Oriente

- Bica
- Gloria
- Lavra

- Aero-Bus 91

- Alverca/Azambuja
- Cascais
- Cacém
- Sintra
- Vila Franca
- Fertagus

- 12
- 15
- 18
- 25
- 28

Stations and lines:

Telheiras

Amadora-Este

Laranjeiras

Colégio Militar

Alto dos Moinhos

Reboleira

Benfica

Sete Rios

Sintra / Cacém / Queluz-Massamá

Sta. Cruz/Damaia

Campolide

Jardim Zoológico

Praça de Espanha

150

25 28

Rua Domingos Sequeira

Estrela

Cç. Estrela/ R. T. Braga

S. Sebastião

under construction

Prazeres

Rua Domingos Sequeira (Estrela)

Cç. Estrela/ R. B. Carneiro

Parque

Torre Tombo

Marquês de Pombal

18

Ajuda

R. J. Deus

R. S. Bento/ Cç. Estrela

R. S. Bento/ Cç. Estrela

Rato

R. Bica Marquês

R. D. Vasco

R. Poiais S. Bento

Boa Hora

R. Buenos Aires

Calçada do Combro

Cç. Boa-Hora

Rua Poço dos Negros

Santa Caterina

Rio Seco

R. S.Domingos á Lapa

Calhariz (Bica

10

Plaça L de Cam

Rua Aliança Operária

R. Garcia Orta

Calhariz

Alto de Santo Amaro

Rua João Barros

Rua S. João Mata

Pavilhão da Ajuda

Santos-O-Velho

Calçada da Tapada

Lar Vito Dam

Alcântara Terra

200

Santos

15

Belém

Hospital Egas Moniz

Rua de Junqueira - C. Congressos

Estação Sto. Amaro

Calvário

Alcântara - Av. 24 Julho

Av. Infante Santo

Cais Rocha

15

Algés

Cascais

20

San

Alcântara Mar

Fogueteiro

Legend (bottom left):

- Interchange
- 25 — Street level interchange with distance in metres
- Torre Tombo — Service stops in one direction only
- Calhariz-Bica — Funicular stations
- 18 Ajuda — Destination

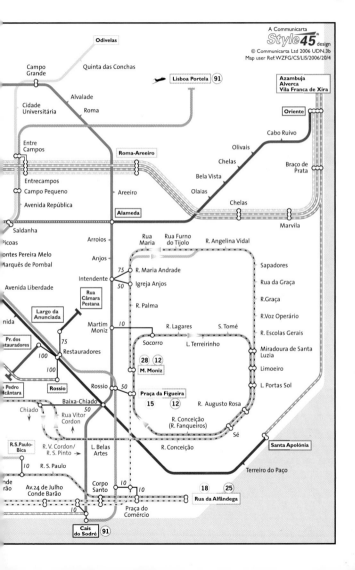

A Communicarta
Style45 design
© Communicarta Ltd 2006 UDN.3b
Map user Ref:WZFG/CS/LIS/2006/20/4

Odivelas

Campo Grande

Quinta das Conchas

Lisboa Portela (91)

Azambuja
Alverca
Vila Franca de Xira

Alvalade

Cidade Universitária

Roma

Oriente

Cabo Ruivo

Entre Campos

Roma-Areeiro

Olivais

Chelas

Braço de Prata

Entrecampos

Campo Pequeno

Avenida República

Areeiro

Bela Vista

Olaias

Chelas

Alameda

Saldanha

Marvila

Picoas

Arroios

Rua Maria

Rua Furno do Tijolo

R. Angelina Vidal

ontes Pereira Melo

Anjos

Sapadores

Marquês de Pombal

Intendente

75 R. Maria Andrade

50 Igreja Anjos

Rua da Graça

Avenida Liberdade

Rua Câmara Pestana

R. Graça

R.Voz Operário

R. Palma

nida

Largo da Anunciada

Martim Moniz

10

R. Lagares

S. Tomé

R. Escolas Gerais

Miradoura de Santa Luzia

Pr. dos staurdores

75

Socorro

L. Terreirinho

100

Restauradores

28 (12)

Limoeiro

100

Pedro cântara

Rossio

50

M. Moniz

L. Portas Sol

Rossio

Baixa-Chiado

Praça da Figueira

15 (12)

R. Augusto Rosa

Chiado

50

Rua Vitor Cordon

R. Conceição (R. Fanqueiros)

R.S.Paulo-Bica

R. V. Cordon/ R. S. Pinto

L. Belas Artes

Sé

Santa Apolónia

R. S. Paulo

10

R. Conceição

nde rão

Av.24 de Julho Conde Barão

Terreiro do Paço

Corpo Santo

10

18 (25)

10

Rua da Alfândega

Praça do Comércio

Cais do Sodré (91)

Lisbon's metro system (ⓦ www.metrolisboa.pt) covers a wide expanse of city. As with the bus, it may be worth buying a travelcard for a day or more.

CAR HIRE

Driving is only the best option if you're planning on exploring some out-of-town places. Car hire in Portugal can be reasonable compared with other countries in western Europe, but for the best rates it's better to book in advance. Several companies operate at the airport, including:

Auto Jardim ⓣ 21 846 2916 ⓦ www.auto-jardim.com

Avis ⓣ 21 843 5550 ⓦ www.avis.com.pt

Budget ⓣ 21 994 2402 ⓦ www.budgetportugal.com

Europcar ⓣ 21 840 1176 ⓦ www.europcar.com

Hertz ⓣ 21 843 8660 ⓦ www.hertz.co.uk

Nacional/Alamo ⓣ 21 848 6191 ⓦ www.guerin.pt

Sixt ⓣ 21 847 0661 ⓦ www.sixt.pt

TRAVEL CARD/LISBOA CARD

The Lisboa Card gives free access to public transport, 26 museums, monuments and discounts at a large number of other attractions. If you don't want to be tied to seeing the attractions but would like to have the freedom of getting around the city, then you can also buy one-day passes in the metro.

⬤ Azulejo *tiles cover many façades in Lisbon*

The Baixa, Chiado & Bairro Alto

Part of the traditional old centre of the city and still very much a focal point for tourists, the Baixa, Chiado and Bairro Alto are also visually quite distinct. Following the destruction of much of the area by the 'Great Earthquake' of 1755, the Baixa (or Baixa Pombalina) was rebuilt by the Marquês de Pombal, who gave it the grid-like structure that can still be seen today. The streets are named after the traders and craftsmen based here since the Age of Discoveries. In the Bairro Alto, the ruins of the Convento do Carmo are testament to the earthquake's ferocity, but the area certainly isn't depressed by it. Along with Chiado, the Bairro Alto is cosmopolitan and renowned for its artistic and literary connections, as well as the numerous fado houses, restaurants and lively nightlife.

SIGHTS & ATTRACTIONS

The pleasant and airy Baixa is easy to navigate from Praça do Comércio to Rossio and is a great place to start exploring the city.

Elevador da Glória (Gloria Lift)

One of the funiculars built to cope with Lisbon's hills, the Elevador da Glória links Restauradores with the Bairro Alto and the Miradouro de São Pedro de Alcântara. It's just a short ride but a steep uphill walk, especially after a day's walking.

ⓐ S. Pedro de Alcântara – Restauradores ⓛ 07.00–24.00 Mon–Thur, until 00.30 Fri–Sat, 08.00–24.00 Sun ⓜ Metro: Rossio

RUA DA GLÓRIA
Coliseu dos Recreios
Socorro
RUA DAS TAPAS
Elevador da Glória
RUA DA MOURARIA
doduro de Pedro de Alcântara
RRO ALTO
PRAÇA DOS RESTAURADORES
Palácio Foz
LARGO DE S. DOMINGOS
o Pedro de cântara
Restauradores
MARTIM MONIZ
Teatro Nacional de Dona Maria II
Estação Central do Rossio
R. DO M. DE PONTE DE LIMA
São Domingos
Igreja de São Roque
Rossio
Museu de Arte Sacra
CALÇADA DO DUQUE
PRAÇA DOM PEDRO IV (ROSSIO)
PRAÇA DA FIGUEIRA
RUA DA PALMA
RUA DAS FARINHAS
RUA DE NOTICIAS
Convento & Museu Arqueológico do Carmo
RUA DA BETESGA
BAIXA
Teatro da Trindade
RUA DA ATALAIA
RUA DA MISERICÓRDIA
RUA NOVA DA
Elevador de Santa Justa
RUA DA SANTA JUSTA
L. A. AMARO DA COSTA
CHIADO
Baixa-Chiado
RUA DOS SAPATEIROS
RUA DOS CORREEIROS
RUA DOS FANQUEIROS
RUA DOS DOURADORES
RUA DA MADALENA
RUA DE SÃO MAMEDE
LARGO D. BARÃO DE QUINTELA
GARRETT
RUA ÁUREA (RUA DO OURO)
R. D. PEDRAS NEGRAS
RUA D. LORETO
PRAÇA LUIS DE CAMÕES
RUA DA PRATA
NICOLAU
CONCEIÇÃO
RUA DA HORTA SECA
RUA CAPELO
RUA DO CRUCIFIXO
RUA DE SÃO JULIÃO
Teatro São Luiz
Teatro Nacional de São Carlos
Governo Civil
RUA DE SÃO FRANCISCO
RUA DA CONCEIÇÃO
RUA DO COMERCIO
R. DA ALFANDEGA
Museu do Chiado
douro de nta Catarina
M. Nacional de Arte Contemporânea
Câmara Municipal
Ministério da Justiça
CORDON
RUA VITOR
RUA DO ARSENAL
PRAÇA DO COMERCIO
NOVA DO CARVALHO
R. D. CORPO SANTO
PRAÇA DUQUE DE TERCEIRA
AVENIDA DA RIBEIRA DAS NAUS
Estação Cais do Sodré
CAIS DO SODRÉ
Cais do Sodré

The Baixa, Chiado & Biarro Alto

0 ———— 500 metres
0 ———— 500 yards

N

M	Metro Stop
✝	Cathedral
🚌	Coach Stn
🚓	Police Stn
i	Information
✈	Airport
🚉	Railway Stn
✚	Hospital

Elevador de Santa Justa (Santa Justa lift)

At the junction of Rua do Ouro and Rua Santa Justa, the Elevador de Santa Justa is an interesting iron structure, built in the early 20th century by French architect Raoul Mesnier du Ponsard, who was a student of Gustave Eiffel. It links the Baixa with the Bairro Alto and there's a viewing tower and café at the top.

ⓐ Largo do Carmo – Rúa do Ouro ⏱ 09.00–21.00 Mon–Sun Ⓝ Metro: Baixa-Chiado; Tram: 28

Praça do Comércio (Commerce Square)

Located at the south entrance to the Baixa, locals sometimes call this wide-open square by its old name, Terreiro de Paço, because of the Paços da Ribeira royal palace that stood here before the earthquake of 1755. It also has the nickname of Black Horse Square, due to the bronze statue of Dom José I (king at that time) that stands in the centre (although it's now more green than black). You'll find the Lisbon Welcome Centre here, along with shops and the Martinho de Arcada café, once a favourite meeting place of artists and writers.

Ⓝ Metro: Baixa-Chiado; Tram: 15

Rossio & Praça da Figueira (Rossio & Figueira Squares)

At the north end of the Baixa Pombalina, the Praça da Figueira is the plain Pombaline square, with a statue of Dom João I at the centre – it's a good place to stop for coffee and cake. To the left is Praça Dom Pedro IV, whose statue is also at the centre. However, it's more commonly known as Rossio Square, after the train station on the left-hand side.

Ⓝ Metro: Rossio

⏵ *Beautiful city views from the Elevador de Santa Justa*

Convento & Museu Arqueológico do Carmo (Carmo Convent & Archaeological Museum)

The skeletal ruins of this 14th-century convent church survived the 1755 earthquake. The archaeological museum that occupies the site today has an interesting collection of artefacts dating back to the Visigoths and Romans, as well as pieces found in the Americas.

ⓐ Largo do Carmo ⓣ 21 3460 473 ⓛ May–Sept 10.00–18.00; Oct–Apr until 17.00 ⓝ Metro: Baixa-Chiado; Tram: 28; Lift: Elevador Santa Justa

Igreja de São Roque & Museu de Arte Sacra (São Roque Church & Sacred Art Museum)

Initially constructed in the 16th century, this church was altered over the next few centuries, including the addition of the Chapel of São João (St John). Look out for the different artistic styles, such as the 16th-century *azulejos*, the *trompe-l'oeil* ceiling and paintings by Italian artists. The museum contains a collection of sacred art and relics.

ⓐ Largo Trindade Coelho ⓣ 21 3235 381 ⓛ 10.00–17.00 Tues–Sun ⓝ Metro: Rossio; Lift: Elevador da Glória

Miradouro de São Pedro de Alcântara (São Pedro de Alcântara viewing point)

At the top of the Elevador da Glória is one of the most pleasant viewing points in the city. Peaceful and shaded by trees, you can rest here with a book or your packed lunch, whilst taking in the views across to the Castelo de São Jorge.

ⓐ S. Pedro de Alcântara ⓝ Metro: Rossio; Lift: Elevador da Glória

◐ *Traditional architecture in the Baixa*

Miradouro de Santa Catarina (Santa Catarina Viewing Point)

Further on from the Praça Luís de Camões towards Estrela, the Santa Catarina viewing point is set in a green, tree-lined square. In the centre is a statue of Adamastor, one of the principal characters from *The Lusiads* (see below).

ⓐ Travessa de S. Catarina Ⓝ Tram: 28

Praça Luís de Camões (Luís de Camões Square)

This small square is dedicated to one of Portugal's most renowned poets, Luís de Camões, author of *The Lusiads* (1572), whose narrative follows the journey of Vasco da Gama and is considered to be one of the greatest epic poems. At the centre of the square is a large bronze statue of Camões.

Ⓝ Tram: 28

CULTURE

Museu do Chiado (Chiado Museum)

This former traditionalist museum was redesigned in 1994 by Jean-Michel Wilmotte. With neo-modern architecture of suspended walkways, floors and ceilings, the museum hosts temporary exhibitions, and its impressive collection of paintings, sculptures and drawings spans 1850 to 1960.

CHIADO FIRE

In 1988, the Chiado suffered a catastrophic fire, which destroyed many of the buildings that had been constructed after the 1755 earthquake. Since then it has been rebuilt, including homes, shops and the Museu do Chiado.

📍 Rua Serpa Pinto 4 ☎ 21 3432 148 🕐 10.00–18.00 Wed–Sun,
14.00–18.00 Tues, 10.00–14.00 Sun & public holidays
🌐 www.museudochiado-ipmuseus.pt Ⓜ Metro: Baixa-Chiado;
Tram: 28

Teatro Nacional de Dona Maria II (Dona Maria II National Theatre)

The Teatro Nacional de Dona Maria II was originally built in the
1840s by Italian architect Fortunato Lodi in a neoclassical style,
and was rebuilt by Rebello de Andrade. There are also guided tours
and a programme of theatre, circus and performance art.
📍 Praça D. Pedro IV ☎ 21 3250 827 Ⓜ Metro: Rossio

Teatro Nacional de São Carlos (São Carlos National Theatre)

Located in the Chiado, the theatre was built in the 18th century
as a replacement for the opera house that stood here before the
earthquake, and includes a neoclassical façade and elaborate rococo
interior. It hosts a busy programme of opera, classical music and
theatre.
📍 Rua Serpa Pinto 9 ☎ 21 3253 045 🌐 www.saocarlos.pt
Ⓜ Metro: Baixa-Chiado; Tram: 28

Teatro São Luíz (São Luíz Theatre)

Opened in 1894, this theatre was once frequented by the 'elegant
classes' of the era, most of whom came to catch a glimpse of the
king and queen, Dom Carlos and Dona Amélia. In 2002 it reopened
following a facelift of its façade and today presents a diverse range
of dance, theatre and music.
📍 Rua António Maria Cardoso 54 ☎ 21 3257 650 🌐 www.egeac.pt
🕐 13.00–19.00, until 22.00 when there's an event
Ⓜ Metro: Baixa-Chiado; Tram: 28

FERNANDO PESSOA

Born in Lisbon in 1888, Fernando Pessoa is Portugal's most celebrated poet. He believed texts should be appreciated for themselves and not for the author, and so began to write under pseudonyms (as himself) and heteronyms (as an alter-ego). Much of his work – more than 25,000 pieces of writing – remained unpublished until after his death in 1935. Lisbon was at the heart of his writing, including his major prose work, *The Book of Disquietude,* and *Lisbon: What the Tourist Should See* (1992). Other notable works include *Poesías de Alvaro Campos* (1944), *Odes to Ricardo Reis* (1946) and *Cartas de Amor* (1988).

RETAIL THERAPY

The Baixa is one of the most traditional and pleasant shopping areas in the city with international chains such as Zara, Mango, Benetton and Levis, as well as a few local stores selling leather goods and jewellery. Look out for the names of the streets, which reflect the traders and craftsmen that worked here for hundreds of years. In the Praça do Comércio you'll also find a parade of shops, including some local crafts. Just round the corner in the renovated Chiado, there are trendy clothes shops, bookstores such as FNAC, and designer boutiques.

TAKING A BREAK

The Baixa, Bairro Alto and Chiado are all renowned for being hangouts for artistic types, particularly the Cais do Sodré area.

Amo te Chiado £ ❶ You can pick up local listings here for clubs and bars in the Bairro Alto. ⓐ Calçada Nova de S Francisco 2 ☎ 21 342 0668 🕘 08.00–02.00 Mon–Sat ⓦ http://amote.clix.pt/chiado.html ⓜ Metro: Baixa-Chiado

Café Heróis £ ❷ Located in the renovated Chiado along Calçada do Sacramento. ⓐ Calçada do Sacramento 14 ☎ 21 342 0077 🕘 12.00–02.00 Mon–Sat, 17.00–02.00 Sun ⓜ Metro: Baixa-Chiado

A Brasileira (do Chiado) ££ ❸ This place is a must. It's easily recognised by the seated bronze statue of Fernando Pessoa outside. ⓐ Rua Garrett 100–122 ☎ 21 3469 541 ⓦ www.abrasileira.pt 🕘 08.00–02.00 Mon–Sun ⓜ Metro: Baixa-Chiado

Suiça ££ ❹ Enjoys outdoor seating and its cakes are considered some of the best in Lisbon. ⓐ Praça D Pedro IV 96–122 ☎ 21 321 4090 🕘 07.00–21.30 Mon–Sun ⓦ www.casasuica.pt ⓜ Metro: Rossio

Café Martinho da Arcada £££ ❺ It can be crowded with tourists jostling for a seat. ⓐ Praça do Comércio 7 ☎ 21 887 9259 🕘 08.00–23.00 Mon–Sat ⓜ Metro: Baixa-Chiado

AFTER DARK

The Bairro Alto has long been a favourite for eating, drinking and dancing in Lisbon.

Restaurants & fado houses
Cervejaria Trindade £ ❻ Housed in a beautiful old canteen once used by the Trinos monks from 1283–1755, it has been a *cervejaria*

(café/bar) since the 19th century. Relaxed and friendly, it's great for steaks and seafood. ⓐ Rua Nova da Trindade 20 ❶ 21 342 3506 ⓦ www.cervejariatrindade.pt ❶ 09.00–02.00 Mon–Sun

Adega Mesquita ££ ❼ Traditional but restored fado house that serves up tasty Portuguese cuisine. Choose from a menu of kid, cod, squid, rabbit and beef. ⓐ Rua Diário de Noticias 107 ❶ 21 321 9280 ❶ 20.00–02.00 Mon–Sat

Arcadas do Faia ££ ❽ Fado house renowned for its authentic but expensive cuisine. ⓐ Rua Barroca 54–56 ❶ 21 342 6742 ⓦ www.ofaia.com ❶ 20.00–02.00 Mon–Sat

Belcanto £££ ❾ Classic Portuguese restaurant famous for its egg dish, *Ovos a Professor*. Aimed at business people, most people are dressed smartly. ⓐ Largo de S. Carlos 10 ❶ 21 342 0607 ❶ 12.00–17.00 & 19.00–23.00 Mon–Sun

Café Luso £££ ❿ One of Lisbon's oldest and most typical restaurants and fado houses, dating back to 1927, a local folk group performs every evening except Thursday, which is jazz night. ⓐ Tv da Queimada 10 ❶ 21 342 6742 ❶ 20.00–03.00 Mon–Sat

Pap' Açorda £££ ⓫ Named after a lobster dish, this is one of the most famous restaurants in Lisbon. Have a drink at the marble-topped bar before enjoying the menu from the Alentejo region, particularly shellfish. ⓐ Rua da Atalaia 57–59 ❶ 21 346 4811 ❶ 12.30–14.30 & 20.00–23.00 Tues–Sat

◀ *Baixa's main street, Rua Augusta, has plenty of restaurants*

Terreiro do Paço £££ **⓬** One of the most highly rated restaurants
in the country and the price reflects that, this restaurant in the
Praça do Comércio is sleek and modern. It has contemporary
versions of Portuguese recipes such as wreck fish from the Azores
with clams, and *bacalhau* with a sauce of olives and coriander.
ⓐ Lisbon Welcome Centre, Praça do Comércio ① 21 031 2850
ⓦ www.terreiropaco.com ① 12.30–15.00 & 20.00–23.00 Tues–Sun

Bars & clubs

Bartis This traditional Portuguese bar, frequented by intellectuals,
is known for its jazz. ⓐ Rua Diário Notícias 95–97 ① 21 342 4795
① 20.00–03.00 Mon–Sun

Café Suave Café-bar with a DJ. The music tends to be a mix of drum
'n' bass, lounge, house and Brazilian rhythms. ⓐ Ria Diário de
Notícias 4–6 ① 21 342 2793 ① 22.00–02.00 Mon–Sun

Capela Housed in a former chapel, this bar/club is usually packed
and plays electronic, dub and groove as well as Madonna and
Kraftwerk. ⓐ Rua Atalaia 45 ① 21 3470 072 ① 22.00–04.00 Mon–Sat

Frágil Classic club that plays a mix of dance music, reggae, samba
and drum 'n' bass. Expect a hot and sweaty crowd. ⓐ Rua da Atalaia
126 ① 21 346 9578 ⓦ www.fragil.com ① 23.30–04.00 Mon–Sun

Ginjinha do Rossio A hole in the wall just round the corner from the
Dona Maria II theatre, this tiny little bar serves nothing but shots of
ginjinha (a cherry-like fruit liqueur), so people grab their drinks and
take them outside. ⓐ Largo São Domingos 8 ① 09.00–22.30
Mon–Sun

Solar do Vinho do Porto Located in an old palace, this is great after a long walk, for a pre-dinner or late-night tipple. Sink into the comfy armchairs and select from 300 varieties of port. ⓐ Rua São Pedro de Alcântara 45 ① 21 347 5707 ② 24.00–07.00 Mon–Sun

Texas Bar Considered to be one of the trendiest hangouts.
ⓐ Rua Nova do Carvalho 24 ① 21 346 3683 ② 23.00–04.00 Mon–Sun

▲ *A view from the Cais do Sodre river walk*

Alfama & Graça

The Alfama is the oldest district in Lisbon, now a clutch of old
houses, churches, squares and narrow cobbled streets that cling to
the hillside just east of the Baixa and sweep down to the Tagus. It
was the Moors that built the first fortified settlement in the city –
the Castelo de São Jorge that crowns the Alfama. The Moors were
driven away by Dom Afonso Henriques in 1147, and the district
became home to royals and the aristocracy. Once they left, the
Alfama fell into decline and has remained an area of patchwork
buildings. Apart from the castle, the district miraculously survived
the 1755 earthquake, though the poverty remained.

SIGHTS & ATTRACTIONS

The easiest way to access the Alfama is by jumping on a No. 28 tram
to the top of the hill. From there it's just a short stroll up to the
Castelo de São Jorge. After your castle visit it's all downhill, in the
best sense, passing the Museu de Artes Decorativas, the Santa Luzia
viewing point, the Sé (Cathedral), through the old Jewish Quarter
and down to the Casa dos Bicos near the riverfront. If you circle
round to the far side of the castle you can visit the Miradouro de
Graça and then the Mosteiro de São Vicente de Fora and the
Panteão Nacional.

Casa dos Bicos (House of the Points)
Take Tram No. 28 to the top of Alfama and then walk down through
the narrow streets, and through the ancient Jewish quarter. Next
to the Casa dos Bicos is a café where you can sit and contemplate
the strange peaked façade. It was built from 1523–30 by Brás de

Alfama & Graça

0 ———————— 250 metres

0 ———————— 250 yards

LARGO DO MONTE
SENHORA DO MONTE
RUA DE SÃO GENS
RUA DAS BEATAS
RUA DO SOL
RUA DA SENHORA DA GLÓRIA
RUA DA BELA VISTA
RUA A AFONSO DOMINGUES
RUA DO VALE DE S. ANTÓNIO
RUA DAMASCENO MONTEIRO
CAL. DO MONTE
RUA DAS OLARIAS
LARGO DAS OLARIAS
RUA LEITE DE VASCONCELOS
TV DA PEREIRA
RUA DA VERÓNICA
RUA ENTREMUROS DO MIRANTE
Convento Nossa Senhora da Graça
Miradouro de Graça
2
RUA DA GRAÇA
LARGO DA GRAÇA
GRAÇA
D. GUIA
MARQUÊS DE PONTE DE LIMA
CALÇADA DE SANTO ANDRÉ
TV. DAS MÓNICAS
CAL. DA GRAÇA
RUA DA VOZ DO OPERÁRIO
CAMPO DE SANTA CLARA
CAMPO DE SANTA CLARA
RUA DO PARAÍSO
COSTA DO CASTELO
LARGO R.D. FREITAS
RUA SÃO VICENTE
Mosteiro de São Vicente de Fora
Igreja de Santa Engrácia/ Panteão Nacional
CALÇADA DE SÃO VICENTE
RUA DOS CAMINHOS DE FERRO
Estação Santa Apolónia
6
Castelo de São Jorge
3
7
R. DE S. CRUZ DO CASTELO
Largo Santa Cruz do Castelo
CALÇADA DO TIJOLO
RUA DE SÃO TOME
RUA DO SALVADOR
RUA DAS ESCOLAS
RUA DOS REMÉDIOS
→ Santa Apolónia
M
Museu Nacional do Azulejo →
Museu de Artes Decorativas
RUA DA REGUEIRA
RUA DE JARDIM TABACO
RUA DE JARDIM TABACO
DO HILAGRE DE SANTA
LARGO DO CONTADOR MOR
4
Miradouro de Santa Luzia
São Miguel
RUA DO LIMOEIRO
RUA DA SAUDADE
RUA DA BARÃO
AVENIDA INFANTE DOM HENRIQUE
RUA DE SÃO MAMEDE
RUA D. SANTO ANTÓNIO
Sé Catedral
ALFAMA
RUA D. TERREIRO D'TREGO
Alfândega
Doca do Jardim do Tabaco
PEDRAS NEGRAS
R. A ROSA
JOÃO D. PRAÇA
8
Igreja da Conceição Velha
Casa dos Bicos
1
RUA DO CAIS DE SANTARÉM
CAMPO DAS CEBOLAS
DA ALFÂNDEGA
AVENIDA INFANTE DOM HENRIQUE
Doca da Marinha
Estação Fluvial
M Terreiro do Paço

N

M .... Metro Stop
🏛 .... Cathedral
🚍 .... Coach Stn
ℹ .... Information
✈ .... Airport
🚆 .... Railway Stn
✚ .... Hospital

Albuquerque, son of the Viceroy of Portuguese India – its location was chosen for its proximity to the shipyards and customs. It now hosts temporary art exhibitions.

ⓐ Rua dos Bacalhoeiros ☏ 21 888 4827 ◷ 09.30–17.00 Mon–Fri
Ⓝ Bus: E18, E25, 37

> **ACTS OF FAITH**
> The Reconquest was not just a battle for territory, but a religious war or Inquisition, in which the Moors were evicted and the Jewish population had to leave or convert to Christianity. Some risked staying and their descendants paid horrifically. By 1540 the first autos-da-fé (acts of faith) had begun, a death penalty for the 'converted' Jewish population and others who didn't follow the Roman Catholic faith. This religious court lasted, albeit less harshly, until 1821. The former Jewish quarter, in the Alfama, has remained poor and claustrophobic, but today it is home to various people, including those from the former Portuguese colonies of Mozambique and Cape Verde.

Castelo de São Jorge (St George's Castle)
One of the most prominent testaments to the city's history, the Moors built the existing battlements in the 8th century. They were driven out in the 12th century and the castle became a royal residence, undergoing various additions, alterations and renovations. Partially destroyed by successive earthquakes, particularly in 1755, it was classified as a National Monument in

◗ *St George stands tall at the top of the hill*

1910 and underwent restoration in the 1940s and 1990s. Surrounded by a dry moat, there's a statue of St George at the entrance. Inside the first square, the Praça das ARAMs, look out for the statue of Afonso Henriques, the first king of Portugal, and take in the panoramic views of the city (look out for the *azulejos*, which tell you what you are looking at).

ⓐ Castelo de São Jorge ⓣ 21 8772 244 ⓦ www.egeac.pt/castelo
ⓛ 09.00–21.00 Mon–Sun Mar–Oct; until 18.00 Mon–Sun Nov–Feb
ⓝ Tram: 28

⬥ *Castelo de São Jorge – the crown jewel of the Alfama district*

Igreja da Conceição Velha (Conceição Velha Church)

If you are walking back towards the Baixa after seeing the Casa dos Bicos, take a look at the doorway of this church. Built on the grounds of a former Jewish synagogue in the 16th century, the church was damaged, like so many buildings, in 1755. What survived and is most notable is the Manueline portal.

Look out for the elaborate symbols of state, religion, nature and discovery that characterise this architectural style, including the Portuguese coat of arms, the Cross of the Order of Christ and the armillary sphere.

Rua da Alfândega ❶ 21 887 0202 ● 08.00–13.00 & 15.00–19.00 Mon–Sun Ⓝ Bus: E18, E25

Igreja de Santa Engrácia/Panteão Nacional (Santa Engrácia Church/National Pantheon)

The church was first built here in the 16th century, but was knocked down after being desecrated in 1630. The replacement church then collapsed after storm damage in 1681. Construction of the replacement wasn't completed until the mid-20th century. The octagonal structure, baroque figurines and main church were designed by architect João Atunes. The dome was added in the 1960s and it was declared the National Pantheon in 1916. Today you can see cenotaphs dedicated to Afonso de Albuquerque (first viceroy of Portuguese India), Henry the Navigator, Vasco da Gama, Pedro Alvares de Cabral (who discovered Brazil), Nuno Alveres Pereira (who secured Portugal's independence from Spain) and Luis de Camões (see page 64). There are also gravestones dedicated to writer Almeida Garrett and fado singer Amalia Rodrigues.

Campo de Santa Clara ❶ 21 885 4820 ● 10.00–17.00 Tues–Sun Ⓝ Bus: 34

Miradouro de Graça (Graça Viewing Point)

This viewing point in Graça, on one of Lisbon's highest hills, is one of the best viewing points in the city. Lined with pine trees, it is a relaxing and romantic spot with views of the castle behind and the city in front. There is also a café here, so you can stop for a rest (see page 81).

ⓐ Lago da Graça ⓝ Tram: 28; Bus: E18, 34

Miradouro de Santa Luzia (Santa Luzia Viewing Point)

This viewing point is recognisable because of the Santa Luzia Church here and the tiled panel depicting Lisbon before the 1755 earthquake. A great place for a breather if it is sunny; if you are walking down hill, go down the steps on the far side of the church (Beco da Corvinha) – here you will see the remains of Moorish walls.

ⓐ Rua do Limoeiro ⓝ Tram: 28

Moteiro de São Vicente de Fora (St Vincent of Fora Church)

Built in the 16th and 17th centuries, and partially damaged in 1755, the church is named after Lisbon's patron saint. You can easily spot its Italian façade and two white towers from the viewing points at the top of the Alfama. The real highlight is the cloisters; added in the 18th century, they are decorated with elaborate *azulejos*.

ⓐ Largo de São Vicente ⓣ 21 882 4400 ⓛ 09.00–12.30 & 15.00–18.00 Mon–Sun ⓝ Bus: 34

Sé (Cathedral)

After liberating the city in the 12th century, Portugal's *Conquistador* and first king, Afonso Henriques, ordered that the cathedral should be built. A mixture of Gothic and Romanesque styles, it didn't come out unscathed from the 1755 earthquake. It was renovated and

today you can go inside and visit its small museum. ⓐ Largo da Sé
ⓝ Bus: E18, E25, 37

CULTURE

Museu de Artes Decorativas (Museum of Decorative Arts)

Housed in a former 17th-century palace, both the building and the
collection were donated by banker and art collector Ricardo do
Espírito Silva to the Portuguese state. Inside you can see an example
of a typical 18th-century aristocratic residence and an important
collection of Portuguese tiles, furniture and textiles.
ⓐ Largo das Portas do Sol ⓣ 21 8814 600 ⓝ Tram: 28

Museu Nacional do Azulejo (National Tile Museum)

Located east of the Alfama along the riverfront, this museum in a
former convent has one of the most important collections of
azulejos in the world. Dating from the 15th century to the present,
the tiles reflect both the cultural and political history of the city and
the country, from the early geometric patterns of the Moorish tiles
to the modernist ones found in the metro station.
ⓐ Rua da Madre de Deus ⓣ 21 814 7747 ⓛ 10.00–18.00 Wed–Sun,
14.00–18.00 Tues ⓝ Bus: 18, 42

RETAIL THERAPY

The Alfama is not renowned for shopping, but if you like
rummaging for a bargain, then head to Feira da Ladra market, which
takes place every Tuesday and Saturday. The market is an array of
household goods, bric-a-brac and the occasional antique. Go early so
you can grab the best bargains.

TAKING A BREAK

With so many fabulous views of the city, the Alfama is an ideal place to stop for some refreshment.

Adega do Atúm £ ❶ (café by Casa dos Bicos) Refreshment whilst contemplating the unusual exterior of the building ⓐ Rua Bacalhoeiros 8c ❶ 21 887 0319 ❶ 12.00–15.00 & 19.00–22.30 Mon–Sun ⓝ Metro: Baixa-Chiado/Cais do Sodré

Café Esplanada da Graça £ ❷ Have a drink in the shade surrounded by pine trees, with a castle backdrop and views across to the Baixa and Bairro Alto. ⓐ Esplanada da Graça ❶ no tel ❶ 10.00–02.00 Mon–Sun ⓝ Tram: 28; Bus: 37

Cafetaria do Castelo de São Jorge £ ❸ Plenty of outdoor shaded seating. ⓐ Castelo de São Jorge ❶ 21 880 0620 ❶ Mar–Oct 09.00–21.00 Mon–Sun; Nov–Feb until 18.00 Mon–Sun ⓝ Tram 28; Bus: 37

Cerca Moura £ ❹ A favourite with locals in the early evening before going out. It offers great views over the Alfama rooftops to the Tagus. ⓐ Largo das Portas do Sol ❶ 21 887 4859 ❶ 16.00–02.00 ⓝ Tram: 28

AFTER DARK

Although not the main area for clubbing and dining in Lisbon, there are still some excellent options here. As the roads are dark

◀ *You might be glad of a tram to climb Alfama's hills*

and narrow, this can be off-putting, so if it is late either grab a taxi or go in a group.

Restaurants

Dragão do Alfama £ ❺ Serves typical Portuguese food such as fried squid and plates of *presunto* (smoked ham). Live fado music every Thursday, Friday and Saturday. ⓐ Rua Guilherme Braga (by Largo de Sto Estevão) ❶ 21 886 7737 ❷ 08.00–24.00 Mon–Sun

Bica do Sapato ££ ❻ Part-owned by actor John Malkovich, this restaurant is a warehouse conversion that attracts local celebrities. Overlooking the river, it serves Portuguese and international food and upstairs has a sushi bar.
ⓐ Avenida Infante D. Henrique ❶ 21 881 0320 ❷ 12.00–14.30 & 20.00–23.30 Mon–Sun

Casa de Leão £££ ❼ With its superb location in the grounds of the Castelo de São Jorge, this restaurant is perfect for both business lunches and intimate dinners, and has great views over the city.
ⓐ Castelo de S Jorge ❶ 21 887 5962 ❷ 12.30–15.00 & 20.00–22.00 Mon–Sun

Clube de Fado £££ ❾ This fado house is located near the Sé (Cathedral) in the heart of the Alfama, in an old but well-maintained building with columns, arches and even a Moorish well in the corner. A very traditional way to enjoy good Portuguese food and hear some of the best fado in the area where it first emerged. The owner, Mario Pacheco, is also one of the musicians, and performs nightly with other musicians. ⓐ Rua S João da Praça ❶ 21 885 2704 ❷ 19.00–02.00 Mon–Sun

Bars & clubs

Chapitô Owned by a Belgian-German partnership, Chapitô is a creative space, a training school for performance arts, a theatre-cum-bar and a restaurant with a terrace. Located near the castle, it overlooks the city and can be an entertaining hangout for a few hours in the evening. It's great for snacks but don't rely on the full menu always being on offer. ⓐ Rua Costa do Castelo 7 ⓣ 21 886 7334 ⓛ 21.00–02.00 Mon–Sun ⓦ www.chapito.org

Lux Bar (and club) Legendary dance club that plays 1980s house, drum 'n' bass and hip-hop, Lux is cool, stylish and impressive with large chairs and beds to slouch on and a birdcage to dance in, as well as a roof terrace. Located in a converted warehouse near Santa Apolonia station, its main bar, club and video bar have different DJs every Thursday, Friday and Saturday, from local to top international names. Early arrival recommended. ⓐ Avenida Infante D. Henrique ⓣ 21 840 4977 ⓛ 18.00–07.00 Mon–Sun ⓦ www.luxfragil.com

▲ Grab a newspaper, find a coffee shop, and soak up the old town's atmosphere

North of the Centre

This chapter covers the area from Praça dos Restauradores just north of the Baixa up to the Estádio da Luz football ground and the Colombo shopping centre – and from the Praça Duquade Saldana west to the Parque Florestal do Monsanto. The Avenida da Liberdade is one of the central arteries of the city and the Praça Marquês de Pombal is considered the 'very centre' of the city because other main roads radiate out from it. From Pombal to Amoreiras and north of Parque Eduardo VII the main focus is the business district, but there are also plenty of attractions, museums, palaces and gardens.

SIGHTS & ATTRACTIONS

Avenida da Liberdade

This attractive avenue, built in the style of a French boulevard, offers a pleasant walk from the Praça dos Restauradores to the Praça Marquês de Pombal. It is lined with elegant buildings, such as the 1920s Tivoli cinema, the remodelled 1930s Tivoli Lisboa hotel and the 19th-century Cinemateca Portuguesa (just behind the hotel on Rua Barata Salgueiro). Designer shops are dotted along its length, along with restaurants and cafés in the shade.

Ⓝ Metro: Rossio/Restauradores/Marquês de Pomba; Bus: 2, 9, 11, 32, 36, 55, 59

Estadio da Luz (Stadium of Light)

This is the largest stadium in the country and the home ground for SL Benfica. The stadium also has facilities for basketball, roller hockey, volleyball, five-a-side football, billiards and badminton.

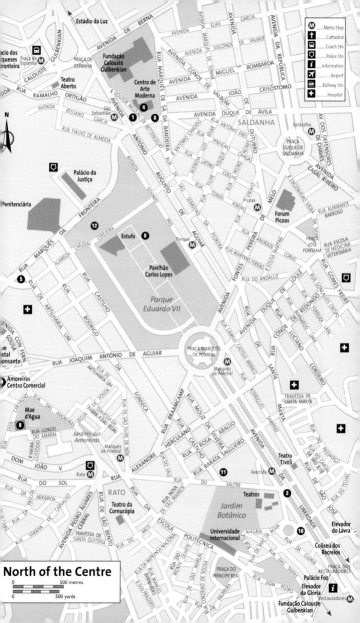

North of the Centre

🅐 Avenida General Norton de Matos ☎ 21 721 9555
🆆 www.slbenfica.pt 🅜 Metro: Colegio Militar/Alto dos Moinhos;
Bus: 54, 68

Jardim Botânico (Botanical Gardens)

Located in the grounds of Lisbon University's Faculty of Sciences,
these gardens have the largest number of tall palms (*cicas*) in the
country, along with numerous rare tropical flora, from palms to
cacti, as well as fleshy plants.

🅐 Calçada da Ajuda ☎ 21 362 2503 🕐 09.00–18.00 Thur–Tues
🅜 Metro: Rato/Restauradores; Bus: 8, 49, 58

🔺 *An avenue of tranquillity at Jardim Botânico*

Jardim das Amoreiras & Mae D'Agua (Amoreiras Gardens)

Inaugurated by the Marquês de Pombal in 1759, the Jardim das Amoreiras was filled with *amoreiras* – mulberry trees that were intended to boost the silk industry nearby. Today there are still some mulberry trees here, along with nine other species. At the back of the garden is the Mae D'Agua, a 19th-century reservoir decorated with *azulejos*.

ⓐ Rua das Amoreiras Ⓝ Metro: Rato; Bus: 8, 49, 58

Palácio dos Marqueses de Fronteira (Marqueses de Fronteira Palace)

This 17th-century palace is considered one of the finest examples of palatial architecture from the period. On a tour of the palace you can see 17th-century mannerist architecture, baroque decoration and some fine examples of 17th- and 18th-century tiles. The formal gardens are geometric in style and filled with fountains and ponds, statues and still more tiles, this time illustrated with mythological scenes.

ⓐ Largo São Domingos de Benfica 1 🕿 21 778 2023 🕒 guided tours 10.30–11.00 & 11.00–12.00 Mon–Sun June–Sept; 11.00–12.00 Mon–Sun Oct–May Ⓝ Metro: Alto doe Moinhos; Bus: 54, 68

Parque Eduardo VII (Edward VII Park)

Named after King Edward VII, who visited Lisbon in 1903, this park lies on a slope at the top end of the Avenida da Liberdade. A network of pathways runs between green lawns, and you can visit the Estufa Fria and Estufa Quente, greenhouses with an array of exotic and rare plants.

ⓐ Parque Eduardo VII 🕒 09.00–19.30 Apr–Sept; 09.00–16.30 Oct–Mar Ⓝ Metro: Marquês de Pombal/Parque; Bus: 2, 9, 11, 32, 36, 55, 59

Parque Florestal de Monsanto (Monsanto Forestal Park)

This park is Lisbon's biggest green space and it is better to explore it by car, as it is not really appropriate to walk around, both for safety and size. Within the vast expanse of the park, there is a campsite, mini-golf, tennis courts, swimming pool, an amphitheatre, shops and restaurant, as well as an exhibition centre and activities for children.

🅰 Estra Barcal, Monte das Perdizes Ⓝ Bus: 11, 14, 23, 24, 29, 43, 48, 70

Praça do Principe Real (Principe Real Square)

In this large, romantic square you can relax on the benches in the shade or have a drink in the café. There is also a children's play area and an underground museum, the Reservatório da Patriarcal.

Ⓝ Metro: Rossio; Bus: 2, 9, 11, 32, 36, 55, 59

Praça dos Restauradores (Restauradores Square)

Just north of Rossio Square at the bottom end of the Avenida da Liberdade, this large open square is dedicated to those who fought in the War of Restoration. On the left-hand side of the square is a former palace, Palácio Foz, which now houses the ministry of culture as well as the tourist office and shop.

Ⓝ Metro: Restauradores; Bus: 2, 9, 11, 32, 36, 55

Praça Marquês de Pombal (Marquês de Pombal Square)

Named after the man who rebuilt the Baixa following the 1755 earthquake (see page 58), this double roundabout is the very centre of the city. From here main roads radiate out to different parts of the city, including south to the old city and the river, west to the business district and on to Sintra, and northeast towards the airport.

Ⓝ Metro: Marques de Pombal; Bus: 2, 9, 11, 32, 36, 55

CULTURE

Coliseu dos Recreios (Recreios Coliseum)

The Coliseum was originally built in 1890 but renovated in 1994 when Lisbon was European City of Culture. You can see both classical and popular music concerts here.

ⓐ Rua Portas de Antão ❶ 21 346 1997 ⓦ www.coliseulisboa.com
🕐 Box Office 13.00–19.30 Mon–Sat (closes half an hour before start time) Ⓜ Metro: Restauradores; Bus: 2, 8, 9, 11, 32, 34, 36, 55, 59, 60

Fundação Calouste Gulbenkian (Calouste Gulbenkian Foundation)

Portugal's most important cultural institution was conceived by Calouste Sarkis Gulbenkian in 1953 (see below). It comprises the country's most prestigious orchestra and choir, as well as museums, exhibition spaces, auditorium, arts library and lush gardens.

The **Orchestra Gulbenkian** has an annual season of concerts at home as well as touring internationally. The **Coro Gulbenkian** is a choir of more than 100 voices. It performs in a range of styles, from a cappella using a few choir members to large-scale performances, in conjunction with the Orchestra Gulbenkian.

The **Museu Calouste Gulbenkian** (ⓦ www.museu.gulbenkian.pt) includes pieces collected by its founder throughout his lifetime.

> **MUSEU GULBENKIAN**
> Calouste Sarkis Gulbenkian (1869–1955) was the son of a merchant family of Armenian origins, who made his own fortune through investments in a Turkish Petroleum company. During his life-long passion for the arts he built up an impressive collection, which can now be seen in the Museu Gulbenkian.

This is a real treasure trove, so you could spend quite some time here. It is organised geographically and chronologically, so you can explore the global treasures in two different circuits.

The **Centro de Arte Moderna José de Azeredo Perdigão** (CAMJAP), Gulbenkian's modern art museum (ⓦ www.camjap.gulbenkian.pt), was founded in 1983 but its collection comprises work acquired by the foundation since the 1950s. The most representative Portuguese artists from the 20th century are included, as well as some

◒ *Sitting proudly outside the Museu Gulbenkian*

international modernist pieces. Highlights include works by Sonia and Robert Delaunay, Arpad, Pablo Gargallo, Henry Moore, Gilbert & George, and Antony Gormley, among others.

🅰 Foundation and Museum, Avenida da Berna; CAMJAP, Rua Dr Nicolau de Bettencourt 🅣 Tickets 21 782 3700; museum 21 782 3461; CAMJAP 21 782 3474 🅦 www.gulbenkian.pt; tickets www.bilheteira.gulbenkian.pt 🅝 Metro: São Sebastião/Praça de Espanha; Bus: 31, 46

Teatro Aberto (Aberto Theatre)

Founded in 1982 by a group of theatre professionals, Teatro Aberto puts on fringe performances by its resident Novo Grupo de Teatro as well as companies from around the country and overseas.

🅐 Praça de Espanha 🅣 21 797 0969 🅦 www.teatroaberto.com
🅝 Metro: Praça de Espanha; Bus: 31, 46

Teatro Tivoli (Tivoli Theatre)

Designed by Paul Rino, the Tivoli was a cinema from when it opened in 1924 until 1988. Today it still has a screen but is primarily used for theatrical productions.

🅐 Avenida da Liberdade 188 🅣 21 357 2025 🅦 www.teatro-tivoli.com
🅝 Metro: Restauradores/Tivoli; Bus: 2, 9, 11, 32, 36, 55, 59

RETAIL THERAPY

Avenida da Liberdade has plenty of designer boutiques, such as Adolfo Dominguez, Armani, Burberry and Massimo Dutti. Amoreiras is one of the older shopping centres but handy if you are staying in the business district, and it still has around 250 quality shops, a ten-screen cinema, supermarket, restaurants and parking. If you want a full-on shopping day, take the metro to Colégio Militar for the Colombo, which has 400 wide-ranging stores with smart boutiques and trendier shops. For something more traditional, Campo de Ourique has most of the international stores found in the shopping centres as well as local leather products and jewellery. There is a branch of the Spanish department store El Corte Inglés at Alto del Parque Eduardo VII, where you can find everything from clothes to stationery, as well as a supermarket.

● *Not just shops, but architecture and statues on Avenida da Liberdade*

TAKING A BREAK

You won't have to walk far to find a café along the Avenida da Liberdade or in Parque Eduardo VII. Many cafés have gardens and a play area for children nearby.

Cafetaria do CAMJAP (Gulbenkian) **£** **❶** ⓐ Rua Nicolau de Bettencourt ❶ 21 782 3474 ⓦ www.camjap.gulbenkian.pt ⓛ 10.00–18.00 Tues–Sun

Esplanada do Principe Real £ **❷** ⓐ Praça do Principe Real ⓛ 12.30–22.30 Mon–Sun ⓝ Bus: 58, 100

Shopping Centres £–££ **❸** All venues are a good option for lunch or coffee and a pastry: **Colombo** ⓐ Avenida Lusiada ❶ 21 711 3600 ⓦ www.colombo.pt ⓛ 10.00–24.00 Mon–Sun ⓝ Metro: Colégio Militar; **Amoreiras** ⓐ Rua Carlos Alberto da Mota Pinto ❶ 21 381 0200 ⓦ www.amoreiras.com ⓛ 10.00–24.00 Mon–Sun

AFTER DARK

There are some quality restaurants to be found along Avenida da Liberdade as well as around Parque Eduardo VII and Rato. There are also some decent eateries in the Amoreiras shopping centre – it is not limited to fast food.

Restaurants

A Valenciana £ **❹** Renowned for its charcoal-grilled meat and chicken, there is also fish on the menu. It is quite cheap, which makes this a good budget lunch. ⓐ Rua Marquês de Fronteira 157 ❶ 21 388 4926 ⓛ 11.00–23.30 Mon–Sun

Botequim do Rei £ ❺ Serves a fine selection of regional Portuguese cuisine with an à la carte menu and a buffet at reasonable prices. ⓐ Alto do Parque Eduardo VII, Alameda Cardeal Cerejeira ⓣ 21 316 0891 ⓦ http://botequimdorei.restaunet.pt ⓛ 10.00–22.00 Tues–Sun

Cantinho Regional £ ❻ Located inside the Amoreiras shopping centre, Cantinho Regional has a menu of mostly sausage dishes from the Beiras region of Portugal, including smoked sausage served in red wine, lamb and rice sausage, as well as a selection of regional cheeses. ⓐ CC Amoreiras, 2nd floor ⓣ 21 383 1631 ⓦ http://cantinhoregional.restaunet.pt ⓛ 10.00–24.00 Mon–Sun

Mãe d'Agua ££ ❼ Located above the aqueduct, this restaurant offers fabulous views across the city and serves a Portuguese and international menu. ⓐ Jardim Amoreiras ⓣ 21 385 8743 ⓛ 12.30–15.00 & 19.00–23.00 Mon–Fri, 19.00–23.00 Sat

O Madeirense ££ ❽ Lisbon's only Madeiran restaurant, this is popular for business lunches. You can try some of the most typical dishes from Madeira, including a *caldeira* (fish soup), tuna, swordfish and *espetada* (skewers of meat or fish). ⓐ Amoreiras Shopping Centre, Av. Engenheiro Duarte Pacheco ⓣ 21 381 3147 ⓛ 12.30–15.30 & 19.30–22.30 Mon–Sun

Quebra Mar ££ ❾ Renowned for its fresh fish and seafood, specialities include monkfish rice, the shellfish plate and grilled sea bass or squid. It also serves grilled meats and steaks as well as salads and soups. Early arrival recommended. ⓐ Avenida da Liberdade 77 ⓣ 21 346 4855 ⓦ http://quebra-mar.restaunet.pt ⓛ 12.00–01.00

Varanda da União ££ ❿ Panoramic city views over the rooftops to the river. The menu is mainly Portuguese with house specialities including stuffed codfish and veal with lobster Varanda style. There is usually a pianist playing during dinner. ⓐ Castilho 14-C, 7th floor ① 21 314 1045 ⓛ 12.30–15.00 & 19.30–23.30 Mon–Fri, 19.30–23.30 Sat

Restaurant Eleven £££ ⓫ The only Michelin-star restaurant in Lisbon, Eleven has a prime location in the business district by the Amália Rodrigues Gardens. Modern and minimalist, the food is as internationally renowned as its chef, Joachim Koerper, with an innovative menu influenced by Mediterranean flavours. ⓐ Rua Marquês da Fronteira, Jardim Amália ① 21 386 2211 ⓛ 12.30–15.00 & 19.30–23.00 Tues–Sat ⓦ www.restauranteleven.com

Bars & clubs

Hot Clube de Portugal This is a legendary basement jazz venue, with live music on Friday and Saturday. Next door there's a music school, which runs master classes and workshops. ⓐ Praça da Alegria 39 ① 21 346 7369 ⓦ www.hcp.pt ⓛ 23.00–02.00 Tues–Sat

Trumps Spread over two floors, this is the biggest and most popular gay venue in the city. There's a café with music and newspapers, while downstairs is split into the bar (with Brazilian music) and the club (dance music). ⓐ Rua da Imprensa Nacional 104-B ① 21 397 1059 ⓛ 23.00–04.00 Tues–Thur & Sun, 23.00–06.00 Fri & Sat

Belém & West Lisbon

Located on the banks of the Tagus, it was from Belém that many explorers set sail for Africa and the Americas. Many of its attractions are associated with or dedicated to them, including the Mosteiro dos Jerónimos, the Torre de Belém and the Padrão dos Descrobrimentos. Belém has enough museums to keep you busy for several days, but the pick of the bunch has to be the Centro Cultural de Belém with its modern art and design museums.

Walk east along the river and you will come to the 25 de Abril bridge with the statue of Cristo Rei towering above it on the far side of the river. From the bridge onwards you come to the transformed Docas, the former docks that have now become one of the trendiest places to eat, drink and dance in the city. Just west of the docks is one of Portugal's most important museums, the Museu Nacional de Arte Antiga, and north is Estrela where you can see the domes of the Basilica da Estrela and the Palacio de São Bento, where parliament now sits.

SIGHTS & ATTRACTIONS

Basilica da Estrela (Estrela Basilica)

This church was built on the orders of Dona Maria I in the late 18th century. The Basilica can be easily spotted from various viewing points around the city, due to its large white dome and neoclassical façade adorned with statues and columns and two white towers. Inside it is decorated with Portuguese marble and has paintings by Italian masters.

🅐 Praça da Estrela 🅣 21 396 0915 🅛 07.30–13.00 & 15.00–20.00 Mon–Sat, 08.00–14.00 & 15.00–20.00 Sun 🅝 Tram: 28

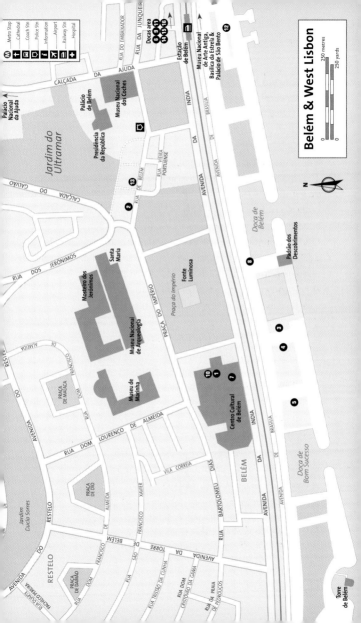

Belém & West Lisbon

Docas area
Estação de Belém

Museu Nacional de Arte Antiga,
Basílica da Estrela &
Palácio de São Bento

Palácio Nacional da Ajuda

CALÇADA DA AJUDA

Palácio de Belém

Presidência da República

Museu Nacional dos Coches

Jardim do Ultramar

CALÇADA DO GALVÃO

RUA DOS JERÓNIMOS

Santa Maria

Mosteiro dos Jerónimos

Museu Nacional de Arqueología

Fonte Luminosa

PRAÇA DO IMPÉRIO

Praça do Império

Padrão dos Descobrimentos

Doca de Belém

RUA DE BELÉM

RUA VIEIRA PORTUENSE

AVENIDA DA ÍNDIA

AVENIDA DE BRASÍLIA

RUA DA JUNQUEIRA

RUA DO EMBAIXADOR

Museu de Marinha

Centro Cultural de Belém

PRAÇA DE MALACA

RUA DOM FRANCISCO DE ALMEIDA

RUA LOURENÇO DE ALMEIDA

VILA CORREIA

PRAÇA DE DIO

RUA BARTOLOMEU DIAS

BELÉM

AVENIDA DA ÍNDIA

AVENIDA DE BRASÍLIA

Doca de Bom Sucesso

AVENIDA DO RESTELO

RESTELO

Jardim Lúcia Sorres

PRAÇA DE DAMÃO

RUA DUARTE PACHECO PEREIRA

AVENIDA DA TORRE DE BELÉM

RUA DOM FRANCISCO

RUA SÃO FRANCISCO XAVIER

RUA TRISTÃO DA CUNHA

RUA CRISTÓVÃO DA GAMA

RUA DA PRAIA DE PEDROUÇOS

Torre de Belém

N

0   250 metres
0   250 yards

- Ⓜ Metro Stop
- ✝ Cathedral
- 🚌 Coach Stn
- ℹ️ Information
- ✈️ Airport
- 🚆 Railway Stn
- 🚔 Police Stn
- ➕ Hospital

Mosteiro dos Jerónimos (Jerónimos Monastery)

At the heart of Belém, this former monastery – now a UNESCO
World Heritage Site – was built on the grounds of a former church
dedicated to the Virgin of Belém. It was later called the Mosteiro dos
Jerónimos after the monks that lived there. Work began in 1501 on
the orders of Dom Manuel I and took almost a century to complete.
The Jerónimos monks resided here for more than two centuries,
giving spiritual help to seafarers and navigators until 1833, when the
order was dissolved. Highlights include the **portals**, which are
adorned with statues and scenes from the lift of São Jerónimo, the
Church of Santa María, with its cross shape, Manueline sculpting
and tombs of Vasco da Gama and Luis di Camões, and the **cloisters**,
a serene place where the monks could meditate.

ⓐ Praça do Império ⓣ 21 362 0034 ⓛ 10.00–17.00 Tues–Sun Oct–Apr;
10.00–18.30 Tues–Sun May–Sept ⓝ Tram: 15

GOLDEN AGE OF DISCOVERY

Portugal's seafaring success really began with Henry the
Navigator, who led an expedition to North Africa in 1415. He
was a leader in navigation and set up a school in the Algarve.
Over the course of the next century, expeditions were sent to
Africa, trade links were set up and islands were colonised –
including the Canary Islands (later transferred to Castile),
Madeira, the Azores, the Cape Verde Islands and São Tomé.
Bartolomeu Dias eventually made it around the Cape of Good
Hope in 1487, and Vasco da Gama opened up the spice trade
route to India in 1498. João Cabral landed in Brazil in 1502 and
trade posts were set up in Mozambique, Angola, Mombasa,
Timor, China and Japan. The last leading maritime figure was
Magellan, who circumnavigated the globe in 1522.

Padrão dos Descobrimentos (Discoveries Monument)

This impressive building is 50 m (164 ft) high and dedicated to Portugal's Golden Age of Discovery. Built by architect José Cotinelli Telmo and sculptor Leopoldo de Almeida, it was inaugurated in 1960 to mark the 500th anniversary of the death of Henry the Navigator. Along the side of the building is a sculpture depicting a Portuguese *caravela* (boat) with the most renowned of the country's seafarers looking out to sea. Henry the Navigator is at the prow, with Vasco da Gama, Pedro Alvares Cabral and Ferdinand Magellan among the other figures. Inside there are exhibition rooms and you can take the lift to the top of the monument for panoramic views of the Tagus and the city.

ⓐ Avenida de Brasilia ❶ 21 303 1950 ❶ 10.00–19.00 Tues–Sun May–Sept; 10.00–18.00 Tues–Sun Oct–Apr ❷ Tram: 15

🔺 *The Mosteiro Jerónimos, viewed from Padrão dos Descobrimentos*

Palácio de Belém (Belém Palace)

Located behind the Museu Nacional dos Coches, you can spy this 16th-century pink palace from the main road. Originally it was a royal summer residence and its beautiful gardens were lapped by the Tagus, before it receded. Today it is the official residence of the President of Portugal and can only be visited by prior arrangement.

ⓐ Calçada da Ajuda ⓣ 21 361 4600 ⓛ by appointment only ⓢ Tram: 15

Palácio de São Bento/Assembleia da República (São Bento Palace/ Assembly of the Republic)

This parliamentary building occupies a former convent. Once a month there are guided tours to see the parts of the convent church and refectory with tiled panels, the grandiose official reception rooms, coats of arms and statues. Tours must be booked in advance.

🔺 *A fitting tribute to Portugal's great explorers, Padrão dos Descobrimentos*

ⓐ Rua de São Bento ❶ 21 391 9625 ⓛ Tours last Sat of the month 14.00 & 15.00 ⓦ www.parlamento.pt/visita ⓝ Tram: 28

Palácio Nacional da Ajuda (Ajuda National Palace)

Take a detour towards the Parque Florestal de Monsanto to see this neoclassical palace, built for the royal family who occupied it from 1861 until 1910. It became a museum in 1938 and holds an important collection of decorative arts from the 15th to the 20th century, including pieces in gold, jewellery, paintings, sculpture, furniture, textiles and ceramics.

ⓐ Largo da Ajuda ❶ 21 363 7095 ⓛ 10.00–17.00 Thur–Tues ⓝ Tram: 15

Torre de Belém (Belém Tower)

This riverside tower was built from 1514–20 as part of a defence system for the River Tague and as homage to Lisbon's patron saint, São Vicente da Fora. It is also a symbol of Portugal's maritime exploits and in 1983 was declared a UNESCO World Heritage Site. You can see some of the best examples of Manueline architecture here (see page 102), particularly the stone ropes that encircle the building, as well as the heraldic emblems, the cross of the Order of Christ and the famous carving of a rhinoceros. If you climb the steps to the top of the tower you will find fabulous city and river views.

ⓐ Avenida de Brasilia ❶ 21 362 0034 ⓛ 10.00–17.00 Tues–Sun Oct–Apr; 10.00–18.30 Tues–Sun May–Sept ⓝ Tram: 15

CULTURE

Centro Cultural de Belém (Belém Cultural Centre)

This modern cultural centre was completed in 1988 and comprises an Exhibition Centre, Performance Centre and Meeting Centre.

The **Meeting Centre** is a high-tech facility that caters for meetings and conferences and includes shops, a restaurant (see page 104), two bars and the CCB's administration centre.

The **Performance Centre** hosts some of the best performances of opera, ballet, classical music, jazz and theatre in the city.

The **Exhibition Centre** comprises four galleries with temporary exhibitions by both Portuguese and internationally renowned modern and contemporary artists. The **Museu do Design** is also housed here, where you can see exhibitions of architecture, design and photography.

ⓐ Praça do Império ☎ 21 361 2400 🕐 Exhibitions 10.00–19.00; other areas of the CCB 08.30–21.45 and until 02.00 when there are performances Ⓝ Tram: 15

Museu de Marinha (Naval Museum)

This museum occupies what were once the north and west wings of the Mosteiro dos Jerónimos. It includes models of boats from the Golden Age of Discovery as well as royal, merchant, fishing and leisure boats.

MANUELINO

Whilst the Reconquest had led to the building of Gothic churches such as the Sé (see page 78), from 1480–1540 a new architectural style emerged. *Manuelino*, or Manueline architecture, named after Dom Manuel I, the king during this period, explored elaborate decoration reflecting themes of maritime voyages, heraldry and religion. Dom Manuel I commissioned numerous buildings, including the Mosteiro dos Jerónimos and Torre de Belém (see pages 98, 101).

ⓐ Praça do Império ⓣ 21 362 0010 ⓛ 10.00–18.00 Tues–Sun
Apr–Sept; until 17.00 Oct–Mar Ⓝ Tram: 15

Museu Nacional de Arqueologia (National Archaeological Museum)
This museum has occupied the former monks' quarters at the
Mosteiro since 1893. Here you can see displays of archaeology,
ethnography, coins, jewellery, stone engravings, sculpture, mosaics
and physical anthropology.
ⓐ Praça do Império ⓣ 21 362 0000 ⓛ 10.00–18.00 Tues–Sun
Ⓝ Tram: 15

Museu Nacional de Arte Antiga (National Museum of Ancient Art)
This museum is also known as the Museu das Janelas Verdes (the
Green Shutter Museum) because of the shutters on the former 17th-
century palace in which it is housed. Highlights include the collection
of Portuguese and European paintings from the 15th to the 19th
century, and religious sculpture from the 18th century. Also look out
for the pieces collected during Portugal's seafaring travels to Africa,
India, China and Japan, dating from the 16th to the 18th century.
ⓐ Rua das Janelas Verdes ⓣ 21 391 2800 ⓛ 10.00–18.00 Wed–Sun,
14.00–18.00 Tues Ⓝ Tram: 15; Bus: 27, 40, 49, 60

Museu Nacional dos Coches (National Coach Museum)
Housed in a former royal riding school, this museum has a collection
of coaches from the 16th to the 19th century, as well as a collection
of oil paintings of the Portuguese royal family.
ⓐ Rua Afonso de Albuquerque ⓣ 21 361 0850 ⓛ 10.00–18.00
Tues–Sun Ⓝ Tram: 15

TAKING A BREAK

This area offers a wide choice of places to stop for lunch. If you fancy a walk along the river, just east past the 25 de Abril bridge is the renovated **Docas** (see opposite), with a large number of cafés, open-air terraces and restaurants.

Cafeteria Quadrante £ ❶ Inside the Centro Cultural de Belém. Generally a hangout for students, whilst overlooking the river near the Doca de Belém. ⓐ CCB, Praça do Império ⓣ 21 362 2888 ⓦ www.ccb.pt ⓛ 08.30–21.45 Mon–Sun ⓝ Tram: 15

Antiga Confeitaria de Belém ££ ❷ Belém's most famous café. Try their *pasteis de Belém* (custard tart), made from a secret recipe dating back centuries. ⓐ Rua de Belém 84–92 ⓣ 21 363 7423 ⓦ www.pasteisdebelem.pt ⓛ 08.00–23.00 Mon–Sat, until 22.00 Sun Nov–Apr; 08.00–24.00 Mon–Sun May–Oct ⓝ Tram: 15

Café In ££ ❸ Typical Portuguese café serving coffee, tea, croissants, cakes, toasted sandwiches and light lunches. ⓐ Avenida Brasileira 311 ⓣ 21 362 6248 ⓛ 12.00–15.00 & 19.30–24.00 Mon–Sun ⓝ Tram: 15

Spazio Evazione ££ ❹ Good coffee and pastries. ⓐ Avenida da Brasilia (by Museu da Electricidade) ⓣ 21 362 4232 ⓛ 12.00–01.00 Mon–Sun ⓝ Tram: 15

Vela Latina ££ ❺ Serves both Portuguese and international food. Good for a light lunch. ⓐ Doca Bom Sucesso ⓣ 21 301 7118 ⓦ www.velalatina.pt ⓛ 12.30–15.00 & 20.00–23.30 Mon–Sun ⓝ Tram: 15

AFTER DARK

Belém's open aspect along with its riverside location makes it a favourite hangout for eating and drinking whilst watching the sunset, before heading out to a club. Back towards the old city are the renovated Docas, by the 25 de Abril bridge, one of the trendiest areas in the city for restaurants, bars and clubs. During the last decade the Docas have been transformed from grim dockland warehouses into one of the most vibrant and trendy areas in the city, brimming with cafés, bars, restaurants and clubs (see numbers 6, 9, 11, 14, 15 and 16) Ⓝ Tram: 15

Restaurants & bars
Alentejanices £ ❻ Spread over three floors and with a terrace, it offers traditional dishes from the Alentejo region, including

▲ *Crossing the Tagus from Belém on a sunny day*

grilled fish and meat dishes as well as desserts. Its wine menu also focuses on the Alentejo as well as a good selection of *vinho verde* (green wine). ⓐ Doca de Santo Amaro ❶ 21 390 8024 ⓦ www.alentejanices.com ⓛ 12.00–24.00 Mon–Sun

Bar do Terraço £ ❼   A popular venue for the arty crowd. Almost every evening during the summer you can come and listen to live jazz and other concerts. ⓐ CCB, Praça do Império ❶ 21 364 8561 ⓦ www.ccb.pt ⓛ 12.30–21.30 Mon–Fri, 12.30–19.00 Sat–Sun

Já Sei £ ❽   This terraced riverside restaurant, next to the Discoveries Monument, is a good budget lunch option with plenty of seafood and fish on the menu, as well as peppered steak and roast lamb. ⓐ Avenida de Brasilia 202 ❶ 21 321 5969 ⓛ 12.30–15.30 & 19.30–23.00 Mon–Fri, 12.30–15.30 Sat–Sun

Tertulia do Tejo £ ❾   Spread over two floors, this relaxed restaurant serves typical Portuguese dishes such as *caldo verde*. Its *pratos do día* (daily specials) offer a quick and relatively cheap lunch option. ⓐ Doca de Santo Amaro ❶ 21 395 5552 ⓛ 12.30–16.00 & 19.30–23.15 Mon–Sun

A Commenda ££ ❿   Located inside the Centro Cultural de Belém, this sophisticated restaurant is renowned for its privileged position overlooking the river, as well as its quality. Although it can be expensive, it prides itself as much on its wines as on its service and menu of traditional Portuguese and creative cuisine. ⓐ CB, Praça do Império ❶ 21 364 8561 ⓦ www.ccb.pt ⓛ 12.30–15.00 & 19.30–22.30 Mon–Sat, 12.30–15.00 Sun

Blues Café £632 ⓫   A mixture of restaurant, bar and club, this popular venue serves Cajun food, has four bars and dedicates nights to jazz, the 1980s, latest releases and Latin music. ⓐ Rua da Cintura do Porto, Edifício 226, Armazém 11 ⓣ 21 395 7085 ⓛ 20.00–03.00 Tues–Sat, restaurant service until 01.00; live bands Wed; disco 01.00–06.00 Fri & Sat

Piazza di Mare £632 ⓬   This Italian restaurant is located between the Discoveries Monument and 25 de Abril bridge. You will find all the old favourites from pizza to pasta to Parma ham and mozzarella and tomato salad – and it won't break the bank. ⓐ Avenida Brasília,

⬤ *Take a tour bus around Belém*

Pavilhão Poente ☎ 21 362 4235 ⓦ www.piazzadimare.com
🕐 12.30–16.00 & 20.00–00.30 Mon–Sun

Rosa dos Mares ££ ⓭   The restaurant is named after a legend
dating back to the Golden Age of Discovery when some sailors,
thinking they were in the middle of the Atlantic, saw roses in the
water (meaning they were close to shore). Today the restaurant even
has a codfish dish named after the 'sea roses', as well as charcoal-
grilled fish and shellfish rice (*arroz de mariscos*). ⓐ Rua de Belém, 110
☎ 21 364 9275 ⓦ http://rosadosmares.restaunet.pt 🕐 12.00–15.00 &
19.00–22.00 Mon–Sun

Speakeasy ££ ⓮   One of the hippest restaurant bars in the Docas.
Serving Portuguese and international food until the club starts.
There's jazz and blues most nights, with a jam session on Mondays
and two or three bands during the week. ⓐ Cais Oficinas, Rocha
Conde Obidos ☎ 21 396 4257 ⓦ www.speakeasy-bar.com
🕐 20.00–03.00 Mon–Thur, until 04.00 Fri & Sat, restaurant service
until 23.00

Uai! ££ ⓯   Brazilian restaurant from the Minas Gerais region with
a menu that includes fried *manioc* (cassava), spare ribs, black beans
and stuffed pumpkin, as well as *caipirinhas* (Brazilian cocktail made
with *cachaça*, limes, sugar and ice). ⓐ Rocha do Conde de Óbidos,
Cais de Oficinas ☎ 21 390 0111 ⓦ http://uai.restaunet.pt
🕐 13.00–15.00 & 20.00–23.00 Tues–Sun (closed lunch Tues & Wed,
closed dinner Sun)

Alcântara Café £££ ⓰   A 1920s-style restaurant in wood, leather
and velvet, this place serves a mixture of Portuguese specialities and

French cuisine. Fish features high on the menu, and there's also a decent wine list. ⓐ Rua Maria Luisa Holstein 13 ⓣ 21 363 7176 ⓛ 20.00–03.00 (restaurant service until 01.00) Mon–Sun

Bars & clubs

Dock's Club Late-night club that's popular with the younger crowd. It has theme nights and 'ladies' nights', with varied sounds from the latest dance and pop to heavy-duty trance. ⓐ Rua da Cintura do Porto de Lisboa 226 ⓣ 21 395 0856 ⓛ 23.00–06.00 Tues–Sat

Indochina Club with a Vietnamese-Oriental theme and one of the trendiest on the Docas. Most popular for its club nights with a mix of pop and the latest dance tunes. Dress to impress or you risk not getting in! ⓐ Rua da Cintura do Porto de Lisboa, Armazém H ⓣ 21 395 5875 ⓛ 23.00–06.00 Tues–Sat

Kremlin A favourite for dance music, this club starts late and stays open until breakfast. ⓐ Rua Escadinhas da Praia 5 (Avda 24 de Julio) ⓣ 21 395 7101 ⓛ 24.00–08.00 Wed–Sat

Op Art Café Located below 25 de Abril bridge, the large windows offer great views of the river. It moves smoothly from café to bar and club, and plays chilled house and dance music. ⓐ Doca de Santo Amaro ⓣ 21 395 6787 ⓛ 23.00–05.00 Mon–Sun

Queens The biggest gay club in Lisbon, and with an enormous dance floor, Queens opens its doors to anyone with any sexual preference. The décor is distinctly 1970s and it has three bars and views of the river. ⓐ Rua Cintura do Porto de Lisboa, Armazém H ⓣ 21 395 5870 ⓛ 23.00–06.00 Tues–Sat

Parque das Nações (Nation's Park)

The Parque das Nações was built for Expo '98 and is a showcase of modern architecture. Stretched along a 3-km (2-mile) length of the Tagus in east Lisbon, there's not a crumbling building in sight. Just a ten-minute bus ride from the airport, and with a major train station, it is here that Portugal travels into the 21st century.

SIGHTS & ATTRACTIONS

The easiest way to get to Parque das Nações is the short metro ride to Oriente. You arrive by the shopping centre and once outside you will see the cable car along the riverfront with the Vasco da Gama bridge at one end, and the Oceanário at the other. In front are the Pavilhão Atlântico and the Doca dos Olivais.

Oceanário de Lisboa (Lisbon Oceanarium)

Located at the south end of the Doca dos Olivais, a visit to the Oceanário is well worth the pricey ticket. Inside is divided into four areas representing coastal habitats of the North Atlantic, Antarctic, Temperate Pacific and Tropical Indian, connected by a central tank to create the illusion that there is one ocean. The Global Ocean is 49 m (160 ft) high and is the centrepiece of the exhibition. You can come face to face with sharks, rays and barracuda, conga eels, giant grouper and tuna, puffins, penguins, seals, seahorses, sea urchins, anemones, corals and jellyfish, to mention just a few.

ⓐ Explanada D Carlos I ❶ 21 891 7002 ❹ Apr–Oct 10.00–19.00 Mon–Sun; Nov–Mar until 18.00 Mon–Sun ⓦ www.oceanario.pt
Ⓜ Metro: Oriente; Bus: 5, 10, 21, 25, 50, 68

Parque das Naçoes

0 ——————— 250 metres
0 ——————— 250 yards

Ponte Vasco da Gama

Torre Vasco da Gama

Video-Estádio

AVENIDA JOÃO PINTO RIBEIRO

AVENIDA DE BOA ESPERANÇA

AVENIDA DO ATLÂNTICO

Feira Internacional de Lisboa

OLIVAIS NORTE

ESTRADA DO MOSCAVIDE

RUA DOUTOR RUI GOMES DE OLIVEIRA

RUA PADRE JOAQUIM ALVES CORREIA

RUA CONSELHEIRO LOPO VAZ

PASSEIO DO CANTÁBRICO

AVENIDA JOÃO II

AVENIDA DOM JOÃO II

AVENIDA DO POLO NORTE

CAMINHO DA ÁGUA

RUA DO BOJADOR

RUA RECÍPROCA

AVENIDA DO INDICO

Pavilhão Atlântico

PASSEIO DAS TAGIDOS

Estação do Oriente

Oriente

Centro Comercial Vasco da Gama

Presidência do Concelho de Ministras

AVENIDA DE BERLIM

Aeroporto de Portela

AVENIDA DO PACIFICO

RUA DO CARIBE

Pavilhão Portuguesa

Doca dos Olivais

AVENIDA DOM JOÃO II

PASSEIO DOBÉLICO

RUA MENDES DA MAIA

PASSEIO DO GONZALO

RUA DO POLO SUL

CAMINHO DA ÁGUA

CAMINHO DA COSTA

Oceanário de Lisboa

PASSEIO DE NEPTUNO

N

Casino de Lisboa

AVENIDA DE PÁDUA

RUA DA CENTIEIRA

AVENIDA DE ULISSES

PASSEIO DE ULISSES

Teleférico

Parque do Cabeço das Rolas

ALAMEDA DOS OCEANOS

RUA PEDRO E INES

RUA NOVA DOS MERCADORES

Pavilhão do Conhecimento

Teatro Camões

CAMINHO DA COSTA

M ....Metro Stop
⌂ ....Cathedral
▤ ....Coach Stn
◉ ....Police Stn
ℹ ....Information
✈ ....Airport
▤ ....Railway Stn
✚ ....Hospital

🔺 *The largest Oceanarium in Europe is in the Parque das Nações*

Pavilhão do Conhecimento (Knowledge Pavilion)

This is an interactive science and technology museum that aims to make science available to all. Highlights include displays on Mathematics, the Flying Bicycle and Nano Technology.

ⓐ Alameda dos Oceanos ☎ 21 891 7171 🅦 www.pavconhecimento.pt
🕐 10.00–18.00 Tues–Fri, 11.00–19.00 Sat–Sun & public holidays
Ⓜ Metro: Oriente; Bus: 5, 10, 21, 25, 50, 68

Teleférico (Cable Car)

If you get a thrill from heights and you don't want to walk the distance between the Oceanarium and the Vasco da Gama Tower, then the cable car is a suitable option. You'll also get a bird's-eye view over the park as you pass the Pavilhão Atlântico (concert venue), the huge Exhibition Centre, restaurants and Vasco da Gama Tower.

ⓐ Doca dos Olivais, Parque das Nações ⓘ 21 896 5823 ⓛ 11.00–20.00 Mon–Fri, 10.00–21.00 Sat & Sun & public holidays ⓜ Metro: Oriente; Bus: 5, 10, 21, 25, 50, 68

Torre Vasco da Gama (Vasco da Gama Tower)

If you feel more comfortable with solid concrete underfoot, then paying to go to the top of the Vasco da Gama Tower might be a better idea than the cable car, although you do get a different aspect from up here. The viewing platform is 105 m (345 ft) high, and what particularly stands out is the view of the Vasco da Gama Bridge as it snakes across the Tagus River.

ⓐ Torre Vasco da Gama, Parque das Nações ⓘ 21 891 8000
ⓛ 10.00–20.00 Mon–Sun ⓜ Metro: Oriente; Bus: 5, 10, 21, 25, 50, 68, 114

CULTURE

Casino de Lisboa (Lisbon Casino)

Aside from the slot machines, roulette, black jack and poker, there's also an auditorium with international and Portuguese music, dance and theatre productions, a lounge bar with live music, several bars linked to the gaming rooms, and three restaurants.

> **PARQUE DAS NAÇÕES CARD**
> This card includes a visit to the Oceanário and Pavilhão de Conhecimento, a single or return trip on the Teleférico, unlimited rides on the tourist train that travels around the park, 20 per cent off bicycle hire at Tejo Bike and 15 per cent off some restaurants. You can purchase the cards from the Oceanário or the Parque das Nações Information Desk.

🏠 Alameda dos Oceanos 📞 21 466 7700 🕐 15.00–03.00 Mon–Sun
📧 info@casinolisboa.org 🚇 Metro: Oriente; Bus: 5, 10, 21, 25, 50, 68

Pavilhão Atlântico (Atlantic Pavilion)

One of the city's major concert and sports venues, this state-of-the-art pavilion is easy to find on the riverfront.
🏠 Rossio dos Olivais 📞 21 891 8409 🌐 www.pavilhaoatlantico.pt
🚇 Metro: Oriente; Bus: 5, 10, 21, 25, 50, 68

Teatro Camões (Camões Theatre)

Home of the National Ballet of Portugal, this theatre's calendar focuses on dance performances by other leading companies.
🏠 Passeio de Neptuno 📞 21 347 4048 🌐 www.cnb.pt 🚇 Metro: Oriente; Bus: 5, 10, 21, 25, 50, 68

RETAIL THERAPY

Centro Comercial Vasco da Gama is the main shopping area. Spread over four floors, it includes fashion stores such as Zara, Mango, Cortefiel, Massimo Dutti, Lacoste and Bershka, as well as shoes, sports, gifts, music, furniture, jewellery and perfume shops. There is also a cinema and a huge supermarket.

There are a few outlets along the Alameda dos Oceanos and Rua da Ilha dos Amores, such as car hire, art galleries, stationery, furniture and toys. There is also a craft shop along Rua da Pimenta.

TAKING A BREAK

There are several places and boutique cafés for coffees and snacks, and plenty of bars if you fancy a gin and tonic with a river view.

Baskin-Robbins £ ❶ In Oriente Station. ⓐ Estação Oriente, Loja G103 ❶ 21 941 9575 🕐 08.00–21.00 Mon–Sun Ⓜ Metro: Oriente; Bus: 5, 28, 44, 50, 210

Café do Parque £ ❷ By the Pavilhão Atlântico, you can stop for a coffee as well as a slice of pizza, sandwich or ice cream. ⓐ Alameda dos Oceanos ❶ 21 894 6109 🕐 10.30–17.00 Mon–Fri, 10.00–18.30 Sat–Sun Ⓜ Metro: Oriente; Bus: 5, 28, 44, 50, 210

Il Caffè di Roma £ ❸ By the Oceanário, an Italian chain of boutique cafés that serve good coffee – you can have it with cream, ice cream or alcohol. ⓐ Edificio Oceanário, Esplanada D Carlos I ❶ no tel 🌐 www.ilcaffediroma.pt 🕐 10.00–20.00 Mon–Sun Ⓜ Metro: Oriente; Bus: 5, 28, 44, 50, 210

Vasco da Gama shopping centre £ ❹ There is no shortage of places to stop for refreshment and a rest from tiring shopping.

⬤ *The exploding fountain in a Parque das Nações street*

AFTER DARK

There is a wide range of restaurants and bars all along the riverfront between the Pavilhão Atlântico and the Torre Vasco da Gama.

Restaurants

100 Norte £ ❾ A restaurant by day and bar-club by night, there is a large terrace and indoor seating. The menu includes steaks, pizza, pasta, fish and sandwiches, as well as a children's menu. The bar-club has karaoke and ladies' nights. ⓐ Rua da Pimenta 105 ⓣ 21 895 8248 ⓦ http://100norte.restaunet.pt/en/index.asp ⓛ 12.00–05.00 Mon–Sun

Café da Palha £ ❻ Caters for large groups and serves traditional Portuguese food. It is particularly good for steaks, grills and salads. They have karaoke and club nights until the early hours of the morning. ⓐ Rua da Pimenta 75 ⓣ 21 895 5915 ⓦ www.cafedapalha.pt ⓛ 16.00–05.00 Sun–Mon & Wed–Thur, 11.00–05.00 Fri & Sat

🔺 *The Teleférico takes you from the Oceanário to the Vasco da Gama Bridge*

Cervejeira Lusitania £ ❼ Typical Portuguese beer and steak restaurant, with a kids' menu. ⓐ Centro Vasco da Gama, 3rd floor ❶ 21 895 8071 ⓦ www.lusitania.com ❶ 11.00–24.00 Mon–Sun

Joshua's Shoarma Grill £ ❽ Fast-food restaurant that serves Israeli and Middle Eastern dishes such as kebabs, hummus, falafel, grilled meats and salads. ⓐ Rua da Pimenta 67–69 ❶ 21 895 6170 ❶ 12.00–01.00 Mon–Sun

Mestre Doce £ ❾ Small family-style restaurant, serving home-cooked Portuguese cuisine such as prawn rice and steaks, as well as good desserts. ⓐ Passeio do Neptuno 3 ❶ 21 894 6043 ❶ 08.00–24.00 Mon–Sun

Sr Frango da Guia £ ❿ Serves grilled Portuguese chicken, typical of the Algarve, and is ideal for a quick lunch. ⓐ Centro Vasco da Gama, 2nd floor ❶ 21 895 1333 ❶ 12.30–24.00 Mon–Sun

El Tapas ££ ⓫ Typically Spanish restaurant serving tapas and main meals. It is located by the Torre de Vasco da Gama. ⓐ Rua da Pimenta 99–101 ❶ 21 896 6900 ⓦ www.el-tapas.com ❶ 12.00–02.00 Mon–Sun

Havana ££ ⓬ Typically Cuban restaurant looking out on to the Vasco da Gama tower and bridge. Specialities include steak Che Guevara, fried prawns and Caribbean salad. ⓐ Rua da Pimenta 115–117 ❶ 21 895 7116 ❶ 12.00–04.00 Mon–Sun

Mar de Sabores ££ ⓭ A Brazilian *rodizio* (grill), where you are given a stop and go sign – when you're ready to eat, waiters serve huge skewers of grilled meats and sausages to accompany your *feijoada*

(black beans), until you display your stop sign. There is often live Brazilian music and a party atmosphere. ⓐ Passeio das Tágides ⓣ 21 892 2750 ⓦ www.mardesabores.pt ⓛ 12.30–23.30 Mon–Sun

Passeio do Oriente ££ ⓮ With a large terrace and two floors inside, it serves traditional Portuguese lunches, dinners and snacks, German beers, sangria, *caipirinhas* and shots. There is also live music, karaoke and Spanish dancing. ⓐ Rua da Pimenta 51 ⓣ 21 895 6147 ⓦ www.passeioriente.com ⓛ 12.00–24.00 Sun–Tues & Thur, until 04.00 Fri & Sat

Senhor Peixe ££ ⓯ Specialises in fish dishes, such as shrimps with garlic to start, shrimp soup, fish stew, lobster rice, grilled squid, grouper or langoustines. They also serve vegetable soup and steaks. ⓐ Rua da Pimenta 35–37 ⓣ 21 895 5892 ⓛ 12.30–15.30 & 19.00–22.30 Mon–Sun

Bars & clubs
Irish & Co £ More of a pub than a restaurant, it serves a strange mixture of Irish and Portuguese food including fresh fish of the day and 'stout' steak, as well as pints of Guinness and Kilkenny. ⓐ Rua da Pimenta 57–61 ⓣ 21 894 0558 ⓛ 12.30–04.00 Mon–Sun

Peter Café Sport £ This bar is a replica of the famous bar in Faial, Azores, where sailors would stop to pick up their messages and have a gin and tonic, or three. If you want something to eat, try the Steak Peter or a toasted sandwich. ⓐ Rua da Pimenta 39–41 ⓣ 21 895 0060 ⓛ 11.00–01.00 Mon–Sun

---

ⓞ *The Praia Grande at Sintra*

OUT OF TOWN
trips

Cascais & Estoril

Just 24 km (15 miles) west of Lisbon, Estoril and Cascais provide the perfect beach and golf locations within easy reach of the capital's culture and attractions. The popularity of the Estoril coast began in 1889 with the opening of the train line from Lisbon. Today surfing and sailing are popular and there are several first-class golf courses, a race track (see page 32), marina and a casino. Popular with kids and the young crowd because of the beach, surfing and clubs, there are also plenty of cultural activities here: picturesque museum-mansions, cultural centres, open-air entertainment and the famous Estoril Casino – as well as the relaxing atmosphere, good seafood and sea air.

GETTING THERE

The Cascais train line runs from Cais do Sodré along the coast via Alcântara Mar and Belém. The journey from Cais do Sodré to Cascais takes 33–40 minutes, from Alcântara 24–31 minutes and from Belém 28–50 minutes, depending on whether you take a fast or slow train. Estoril is two stops before Cascais, so you can deduct 4–5 minutes from the journey time.

SIGHTS & ATTRACTIONS

Boca do Inferno (Mouth of Hell)

This is a 150-million-year-old cavern with steep sides and deep gouges made by the turbulent sea. When it is windy and the sea is quite choppy, it is quite a spectacular sight to see the Boca turn into a mass of bubbling white water. You can reach it by walking west

Cascais & Estoril

| 0 | 250 metres |
| 0 | 250 yards |

- Ⓜ Metro Stop
- ✝ Cathedral
- ▣ Coach Stn
- ▣ Police Stn
- ✈ Airport
- ⓘ Information
- 🚉 Railway Stn
- ✚ Hospital

N

Baía de Cascais

Marina de Cascais

ESTORIL

- RUA DE ANTONIO MARTINS
- BOMBEIROS VOLUNTARIOS
- AVENIDA DOS
- AVENIDA DE PORTUGAL
- ALAMEDA GARRETT
- Correios (Museu)
- Casino Estoril
- AVENIDA CLOTILDE
- RUA S TOME E PRINCIPE
- AVENIDA DE SOUSA
- RUA DE MELO E SOUSA
- AVENIDA AIDA
- MARGINAL
- Estaçao Estoril
- Lisbon & São João de Estoril
- Praia da Poça
- Piscina Oceânica
- Praia de Tamariz
- Praia do Monte Estoril
- Museu da Música
- AVENIDA FAUSTO FIGUEIREDO
- RUA DAS ACACIAS
- AVENIDA DE SABOIA
- AVENIDA MONDARIZ
- AVENIDA DE S PEDRO
- RUA DE PADUA
- AVENIDA DO FAIAL
- AVENIDA DA VENEZUELA
- Parque Palmela
- AVENIDA DA ARGENTINA
- AVENIDA DO BRASIL
- RUA MARECHAL CARMONA
- MARGINAL
- AVENIDA
- Praia da Duquesa
- Praia da Palmela
- Estaçao Cascais
- Praia da Conceiçao
- Praia de Rainha
- Praia da Ribeira
- Estoril Golf
- AVENIDA DE SINTRA
- COSTA PINTO
- AVENIDA TEN CORONEL JOSE PINTO
- Oltavos Golf
- DE ALUDE
- RUA JOSE TEIXEIRA JUNIOR
- AVENIDA ENG ANTONIO DE A COUTINHO
- Centro Comercial Vila Cascais
- RUA VISCONDE DA LUZ
- ALAMEDA COMB DA GRANDE GUERRA
- RUA SEBAST MELLO
- ALAMEDA DUQUESA DE PALMELA
- AVENIDA 25 DE ABRIL
- RUA S.D PEDRO
- R DR FRANCISCO AVILEZ
- R DR JOSE DAZILEZ
- RUA FREIRAS
- AV DOS NAVEGANTES
- CASCAIS 35
- R AV VASCO DA GAMA
- RUA S. SANCHES
- RUA JOSE FLORINDO
- AV DA ULTRAMAR
- RUA GUILHERME FERNANDES
- RUA DE SANTO SILVA
- DA REPUBLICA
- CARLOS I
- Igreja Assunçao
- Cidadela
- Casa de Santa Marta
- Farol de Santa Marta
- Praia Santa Marta
- AVENIDA DON
- RUA M PARACHA
- Centro Cultural de Cascais
- Museu Municipal de Cascais
- Parque Municipal da Gandarinha
- RUA VISCONDE DA GANDARINHA
- AVENIDA REI HUMBERTO DE ITALIA
- Boca do Inferno
- AVENIDA REI ESPIRITO SANTO
- Quinta da Marinha Golf & Oltavos Golf
- Museu do Mar
- Bull Ring
- R JAIME THOMPSON
- AVENIDA ADELINO AMARO DA COSTA
- DE ABRIL
- RUA CARVALHO ARAUJO
- R DR ANTONIO MARTINS
- RUA JOSE JOAQUIM FREIRA
- AVENIDA DE ANTONIO CASTELO BRANCO
- ENG
- Cabo da Roca
- AVENIDA
- R DE SANTANA
- RUA VISCONDE TOJAL
- RUA JOSE REAL
- AVENIDA NOVA
- RUA FRANTILA LAMAS
- R DR JOSE DAZILEZ
- R DE BEM LEMBRADOS
- AVENIDA INFANTE D HENRIQUE

along the coast road, but be careful of going too close, as some people have been swept away.

ⓐ Avenida Rei de Italia, Cascais ⓝ Train: Cascais

Cabo da Roca

West of Cascais, this is the most westerly point in continental Europe. As well as a lighthouse, tourist office and other facilities, this is a great spot for walks and wild and dramatic views.

ⓐ Cabo da Roca, Azóia

Casa de Santa Maria (Santa Maria House)

Built by architect Raúl Lino in the early 20th century, this is a romantic combination of Mediterranean mansion and Moorish revivalist style. Look out for the 17th-century *azulejos* taken from an

ⓞ *You'll need lady luck with you at the Casino Estoril*

old chapel – which depict some quite horrific scenes – the elaborate ceilings and the view from the patio.

ⓐ Estrada do Farol de Santa Marta, Marina de Cascais ① 21 482 5404 ⓛ 10.00–13.00 & 14.00–17.00 Tues–Sun Ⓝ Train: Cascais

Casino Estoril (Estoril Casino)

The largest casino in Europe, this has a theatre-auditorium, restaurants, art gallery and shops, as well as gaming rooms. It is strictly smart dress only (men with a jacket and tie).

ⓐ Praça José Teodoro dos Santos ① 21 466 7700 ⓦ www.casino-estoril.pt ⓛ 15.00–03.00 Mon–Sun Ⓝ Train: Estoril

Espaço Memória dos Exílios (Estoril Post Office Museum)

This is a modernist building designed by Portuguese architect Adelino Nunes and opened in 1942. As Estoril was a haven for many exiles during World War II, the first floor of the post office now has a permanent exhibition on this theme.

ⓐ Avenida Marginal 7152a ① 21 482 5022 ⓛ 09.30–18.30 Mon–Fri, until 12.30 Sat Ⓝ Train: Cascais

Estoril Coast beaches

Most beaches along the Estoril Coast are blue-flag beaches, in recognition of the water quality as well as the nearby infrastructure.

There are beaches and a promenade all the way from Cascais to Estoril. **Praia da Ribeira** by Cascais old town is a focal point because of the fishing boats that arrive here and the craft stalls and music performances, but it is not really a place to go swimming. **Conceição**, **Rainha** and **Duquesa** are small sandy beaches where you can hire sunbeds and grab a drink at one of the nearby bars. In Estoril the beaches include **Monte Estoril**, by the Mirage Cascais

Hotel, and **Tamariz**, which is popular with children, as there are pools of seawater. Further east is **Poça**, a calm and pleasant long beach, but the biggest stretch of sand and best place for watersports is **Carcavelos** near Oeiras. Popular with surfers, particularly in spring and autumn, there are also volleyball and beach football pitches and a roller-skating rink. All have nearby cafés and restaurants.

For something a little more remote, you will have to drive west to Cabo da Roca, the most westerly point in continental Europe, then head north to **Guincho**. Naturally wild, it has a large area of sand dunes, long stretches of sand, and, because of the Atlantic wind, is good for surfing, bodyboarding and windsurfing.

Igreja de Nossa Senhora da Assunção (Nossa Senhora da Assunção Church)

Built in the 16th century, this church includes gilt work on the wooden altar, panels of *azulejos* and the 17th-century paintings of the Annunciation by Josefa de Obidos.

ⓐ Largo da Assunção ⓛ 09.00–13.00 & 17.00–20.00 Mon–Sun
ⓝ Train: Cascais

Marina de Cascais (Cascais Marina)

Cascais marina is a hub of social and sporting activity. Modern and well equipped, there are 650 moorings for boats here, as well as commercial space. Sailing races and regattas regularly start from here, and the sailing school Escola de Vela Tuttamania runs courses. The races are run by the Clube Naval de Cascais (ⓦ www.cncascais.pt). There are also a few shops, restaurants and cafés surrounding the marina.

ⓞ 21 482 4822 ⓦ www.marinacascais.pt ⓝ Train: Cascais

Museu do Mar (Museum of the Sea)

Here you can discover the town's links with the sea and learn something about natural history and underwater archaeology. One of the most interesting parts of the museum includes models of boats and treasure salvaged from shipwrecks found off the coast.

ⓐ Rua Júlio Pereira de Melo, Cascais ⓣ 21 482 5400 ⓛ 10.00–17.00 Tues–Sun ⓝ Train: Cascais

▲ The marina at Cascais

Museu Municipal de Cascais/Palácio dos Condes de Castro Guimarães (Cascais Municipal Museum/Condes de Castro Guimarães Palace)

Housed in the 20th-century former mansion home of Jorge O'Neill, this place has fabulous ocean views. Sold to the Condes de Castro Guimarães in 1910, it underwent some alterations and today reflects the owner's penchant for acquiring art and furniture from various eras, including a neo-Gothic organ. The count died in 1927 and left the house to the local authorities, which turned it into a museum. Officially opened in 1931, there is a rich collection of *azulejos*, porcelain, furniture and a fine library of historic books.

ⓐ Avenida Rei Humberto II de Itália, Parque Marechal Carmona
ⓣ 21 482 5407 ⓛ 10.00–17.00 Tues–Sun ⓝ Train: Cascais

Parque Municipal da Gandarinha (Gandarinha Municipal Park)

This large leafy park stretches from the Condes de Castro Guimarães museum to the Boca de Inferno. It is a pleasant place for a leisurely walk, faces the seafront and is filled with statues, ponds and palms, as well as the Cascais Sports Pavilion and the Manuel Passolo riding school.

ⓐ Avenida Rei Humberto II de Itália ⓝ Train: Cascais

CULTURE

Auditório Fernando Lopes-Graça (Fernando Lopes-Graça Auditorium)

Named after one of the 20th century's famous Portuguese composers, located next to the Hotel Estoril-Sol, this open-air auditorium is used for orchestral concerts, jazz, theatre and fado groups.

ⓐ Parque Palmela, Avenida Marginal ⓣ 21 482 5447 ⓝ Train: Cascais

Centro Cultural de Cascais (Cascais Cultural Centre)
Located on the site of a former 17th-century convent, the buildings
were rebuilt by architect Jorge Silva as an art museum and
exhibition centre. There is also an auditorium here, which is used
for concerts.
ⓐ Avenida Rei Humberto II de Itália, s/n ⓣ 21 484 8900
ⓛ 10.00–20.00 Tues–Sun; exhibitions 12.00–19.00 Tues–Sun
Ⓝ Train: Cascais

**Museu da Música/Casa Verdades de Faria (Music Museum/
Verdades de Faria House)**
Wealthy arts patron, Mantero Belard, left this house to the town
as a house-museum and gardens, and dedicated it to his mother.
Decorated with painted stucco, glass and 17th-century tiles, today
it houses a collection of Portuguese instruments bought from the
Corsican ethnomusicologist Michel Giacometti.
ⓐ Avenida de Sabóia 1146B, Estoril ⓣ 21 482 5405 ⓛ 10.00–13.00 &
14.00–17.00 Tues–Sun Ⓝ Train: Cascais

RETAIL THERAPY

There are craft stalls on the beaches, traditional shopping in
Cascais old town, and a weekly market next to the bullring,
where you can find good-quality leather goods and jewellery.
There is an open-air crafts fair during July and August by Estoril
Casino, selling crafts from all over the country, including ceramics,
tiles and wood-carvings.

Vila Cascais, on Avenida Marginal by the station, is a modern
shopping centre with shops, a supermarket and multiplex cinema.
There is a larger shopping centre, Cascais Shopping, located out of

town towards Sintra on the EN9 road. You can catch buses 406, 417 and 418 from Cascais station.

🔺 *Take a stroll along the promenade at Estoril*

AFTER DARK

Cascais and Estoril have a good range of cafés and restaurants – many with outdoor seating areas – from traditional Portuguese tavernas to international cuisine. Watch out for touristy prices; there are reasonable places to be found. In Largo Luiz de Camões and Rua Frederico Arouca there are several bars and a few fado clubs. There are also a lot of bars around Cascais Marina, and Carcavelos beach is also a popular choice.

Restaurants

Jonas Bar £ ❶ Located on the edge of Tamariz beach, this is a fast-food restaurant-bar where you can have burgers for lunch or stop for a beachfront drink in the evening. ⓐ Paredão, Praia do Tamariz ❶ 21 467 6946 ◐ 08.00–02.00 Mon–Sun May–Sept; until 18.00 Mon–Sun Oct–Apr

Nuts Club £ ❷ A popular club for the younger crowd, located by Cascais Marina, it has several bars, two dance floors, dance music, karaoke and DJs. ⓐ Avenida Rei Humberto II de Itália ❶ 21 484 4109 ◐ 23.30–05.00 Tues–Sat summer; Fri & Sat winter

Restaurante Praia do Tamariz £ ❸ Located by the beach, this is a Spanish restaurant where you can have tapas and paella. ⓐ Praia do Tamariz ❶ 21 468 1010 ◐ 09.00–sunrise the following morning Mon–Sun ⓦ www.restaurantepraiatamariz.com

Casa Mexico ££ ❹ Located in the Marina de Cascais, this bright and cheerful restaurant-bar offers typical Mexican food from *nachos* to *enchiladas*, *burritos* and *tacos*. ⓐ Marina de Cascais, loja 27a

● 21 481 8010 ● 20.00–01.00 Wed–Sat, 13.00–17.00 Sun
ⓦ www.casamexico.pt

Restaurante Cervejaria Luzmar ££ ❺ A typical Portuguese surf 'n'
turf restaurant where you should also try the seafood rice option
(*arroz de marisco*) ⓐ Alameda Combatentes G Guerra 104 ● 21 484
5704 ● 12.00–16.30 & 19.00–24.00 Mon–Sun

Restaurante Rosa Maria ££ ❻ This restaurant serves good
traditional Portuguese cuisine, has excellent sea views and is
located inside the Farol Design Hotel. ⓐ Avenida Rei Humberto II de
Itália 7 ● 21 823 3490 ● 12.30–15.30 & 19.30–23.30 Mon–Sun

ACCOMMODATION

Being a coastal resort area, there is no shortage of accommodation.
For more options try ⓦ www.secretplaces.com &
ⓦ www.estorilcoast-tourism.com

Estalagem Muchaxo £ Located on Guincho beach, just a short
distance from Cascais and Estoril, this is a typical Portuguese
hotel with restaurant, breakfast room, bars, anti-stress centre,
sauna and seawater pool. ⓐ Estrada do Guincho ● 21 487 0221
ⓔ info@muchaxo.com

Hotel Atlântico £ This hotel is popular with both business and
leisure guests, and has two seawater swimming pools, a restaurant
and mini-golf. ⓐ Avenida Marginal 8023 A ● 21 468 0270
ⓔ hotel.atlantico@mail.telepac.pt

Estalagem do Farol – Design Hotel ££ This hotel combines a 19th-century mansion with 21st-century interior design. It is located next to the marina and it has restaurants, bars and a saltwater swimming pool. ⓐ Avenida Rei Humberto II de Italia ⓣ 21 482 3490 ⓔ faroldh@mail.telepac.pt

Hotel Albatroz ££ Situated on the bay, this is one of Portugal's top boutique hotels. A privately owned residence, each of its rooms has a unique character. ⓐ Rua Frederico Arouca 100 ⓣ 21 484 4827 ⓦ www.albatrozhotels.com ⓔ albatroz@albatrozhotels.com

Hotel Cidadela ££ Just 500 m (1,640 ft) from the beach, this modern hotel has a bar, restaurant, swimming pool, poolside bar and barbecue. ⓐ Avenida 25 de Abril ⓣ 21 482 7600 ⓔ hotelcidadela@hotelcidadela.com

Hotel Estoril Eden ££ A large hotel with guest rooms and apartments, it also has an indoor and outdoor swimming pool, jacuzzi, sauna, massage service, sunbeds, restaurant and poolside snack bar. ⓐ Avenida de Sabóia 209 ⓣ 21 466 7600 ⓦ www.hotel-estoril-eden.pt ⓔ geral@hotelestorileden.com

Hotel Quinta da Marinha £££ Perched on the cliff tops facing the sea and with views of the Sintra hills, this resort hotel has two pools, golf course, tennis courts, restaurants and bars. ⓐ Quinta da Marinha ⓣ 21 486 0100 ⓦ www.quintadamarinha.com ⓔ sales@quintadamarinha.com

Sintra

Sintra is great to see if you have more than a couple of days in the Lisbon area. Surrounded by the green and rocky hills of the Serra da Sintra, its palaces, castle, houses and museums are among the country's top attractions. A UNESCO Heritage Site since 1995, the Romans, Moors and Portuguese royal family all adored it here, and with the advent of the Lisbon–Sintra railway in the 19th century it became a summer resort for the middle classes. You can easily walk around the Vila Velha (historic centre), dominated by the Palácio Nacional, but it is easier to take a bus or car to see the Palácio da Pena and some of the other attractions.

Each year Sintra hosts one of the most famous music festivals in the country (see page 10), and the Centro Cultural Olga Cadaval hosts a string of exciting concerts and performances.

GETTING THERE

The Sintra train passes through Oriente and Entrecampos stations in Lisbon and also Queluz. Trains leave every half hour and take 75 minutes from Oriente to Sintra; 39 from Entrecampos. It takes 15 minutes from Entrecampos to Queluz; 28 minutes from Oriente.

Getting around Sintra is easy – a bus (434) runs every 20 minutes from the train station to the historic centre and the Palácio Nacional, the Castelo dos Mouros, Palácio da Pena and back to the station. A rover ticket allows you to hop on and off where you please. Alternatively you can ride in one of the horse-drawn carriages that operate between Sintra and the Serra – you will see these in front of the Palácio Nacional.

SIGHTS & ATTRACTIONS

Castelo dos Mouros (Moors Castle)

Originally built by the Moors around the 8th and 9th centuries in dramatic surroundings on two hills in the Serra de Sintra, the castle was conquered by D Afonso Henriques in the 12th century and rebuilt by D Fernando in the 19th century, when the walls were restored. The walls and turrets of the castle can be seen winding their way around the ridges of the hills, but also see the chapel built by D Afonso with its Romanesque doorways, tracings of paintings and medieval tombs, as well as the Moorish cistern and the 'royal tower'. ⓐ Rua da Pena ⓣ 21 923 7300 (visits) ⓛ 09.00–19.00 1 May–14 June; 09.00–20.00 15 June–15 Sept; 09.00–19.00 16 Sept–31 Oct; 09.30–18.00 1 Nov–30 Apr Ⓝ Train: Sintra; Bus: 434 from Sintra Train Station/Historic Centre

Palácio da Pena (Pena Palace)

Located in the Serra da Sintra on the peak of a rocky hill, this 19th-century palace was built on the orders of D Fernando II. The former monastery had been severely damaged by the 1755 earthquake, but around the remaining Renaissance altar of the chapel, a palace of Moorish, Gothic, Manueline and Renaissance pastiche was built, influenced by the European castles of the time. Don't miss the original 16th-century Manueline cloisters, the odd-shaped sentry boxes, the 18th-century tiles, period furniture and the murals, as well as impressive views across the park and surrounding area.

Ⓝ Train: Sintra; Bus: 434 from Sintra Train Station/Historic Centre

The impressive **Parque da Pena** is a 200-hectare garden surrounding the palace.

ⓐ Estrada da Pena ⓣ 21 910 5340 ⓛ 10.00–19.00 Tues–Sun (summer); until 17.00 Tues–Sun (winter)

Palácio de Seteais (Seteais Palace)

This palace was built in the 18th century. In the 19th century, the 5th Marquis of Marialva added a triumphal arch in honour of the D João VI (then prince regent) and Dona Carlota Joaquina. Today it is a luxury hotel (see page 141) – if you want to see inside, make a reservation.
ⓐ Rua Barbosa du Bocage 8 ⓣ 21 923 3200 ⓝ Train: Sintra; Bus: 434 from Sintra Train Station/Historic Centre

Palácio de Queluz (Queluz Palace)

This pink palace is located between Lisbon and Sintra, so you might like to stop off for a tour. It is often referred to as a 'little Versailles' for its elegance and formal gardens filled with baroque statues. Today the East Wing is the official residence of foreign dignitaries invited by the Portuguese state. Highlights include the façade of the palace, the Music Room, the Throne Room, the collection of Portuguese furniture and the gardens.
ⓐ Largo do Palácio de Queluz ⓣ 21 434 3860 ⓛ Palace 09.30–17.00 Mon–Sun, gardens 10.00–18.00 (summer), 10.00–17.00 (winter) Mon–Sun ⓝ Train: Queluz

Palácio Nacional de Sintra (Sintra National Palace)

As you approach Sintra, look out for the unmistakeable white chimneys of the National Palace, also known as the Paço Real or Palácio da Vila. A mixture of *mudejar* (Arabic-style), Gothic, Manueline and Renaissance styles, it is a national monument.

You cannot fail to admire the stunning *mudejar azulejos* that cover the walls of various halls, patios and the royal chapel. Renaissance

style was added during the reign of D João III (1521–57), who built the Sala dos Cisnes, where you can see various royal portraits. The Sala dos Brasões contains 18th-century tiles by the best masters at the time.

🔺 *You can't miss the unmistakeable chimneys of the Palácio Nacional in Sintra*

ⓐ Large Reina D Amélia ❶ 21 910 6840 🕙 10.00–17.30 Thur–Tues
Ⓝ Train: Sintra; Bus: 434 from Sintra Train Station/Historic Centre

Quinta da Regaleira e Jardins (Regaleira Estate & Gardens)

This fascinating palace and gardens are worth a visit if you are
interested in mystery, mythology and fantasy. It is a beautiful
combination of architectural styles, built at the beginning of the
20th century. Look out for the neo-Gothic, neo-Manueline carved
stone motifs, the labyrinthine gardens, statues, grottoes, waterfalls
and lakes, as well as the dry well with the Templar's cross, eight-
pointed star and a chapel. Underneath is a crypt that leads into a
gallery connecting it to the palace. You can visit the palace and
gardens, but if you want a guided visit you should book ahead.
ⓐ Rua Barbosa du Bocage ❶ 21 910 6650 🕙 10.00–17.30 Wed–Mon
Ⓝ Train: Sintra; Bus: 434 from Sintra Train Station/Historic Centre

Sintra tram

Hop on this tram for a relaxing ride to the wine-growing town of
Banzão, near Colares, and onto Praia das Maças, where you will find
the best-known beach on the Sintra coastline. The tram is near the
Museu de Arte Moderna in Sintra and takes 50 minutes.
❶ 21 923 8789 🕙 Summer Fri–Sun, first tram leaves Sintra at 10.10,
last tram leaves Praia das Maças at 16.45.

CULTURE

Centro Cultural Olga Cadaval (Olga Cadaval Cultural Centre)

This cultural centre was restored and updated after it was damaged
by fire in 1985. Today it hosts concerts, theatre and performing
arts events.

ⓐ Largo Dr Vergilio Horta ⓘ 21 923 8500 ⓒ 14.00–18.00 Mon–Fri, 10.00–13.00 & 14.00–18.00 Sat; booking office closes one hour before event starts ⓝ Train: Sintra; Bus: 434 from Sintra Train Station/Historic Centre

Museu de Arte Moderna (Museum of Modern Art)

This museum is a treat for 20th-century art-lovers. It houses an interesting collection of European and American art. The Berardo Collection, as it is known, includes works by Pablo Picasso, Miró, Max Ernst, Man Ray, George Segal, Andy Warhol and Roy Lichtenstein. ⓐ Avenida Heliodoro Salgado ⓘ 21 924 8170 ⓒ 10.00–18.00 Wed–Sun, 14.00–18.00 Tues ⓝ Train: Sintra; Bus: 434 from Sintra Train Station/Historic Centre

Museu do Brinquedo (Toy Museum)

Here you can see the toy collection of João Arbués Moreira, gathered together over the course of 50 years, from teddy bears and carousels to soldiers and Dinky toys.

⬤ *One of many interesting exhibits from the toy museum*

ⓐ Rua Visconde de Monserrate ⓣ 21 910 6016 ⓛ 10.00–18.00
Tues–Sun ⓝ Train: Sintra; Bus: 434 from Sintra Train Station/Historic
Centre

RETAIL THERAPY

Don't expect large state-of-the art shopping centres in the middle
of Sintra. Wander the tangle of streets of the Vila Velha and you are
bound to find some treasures, from local crafts, traditional
instruments and antiques to books, pottery and wine. The Loja do
Arco (Rua Arco do Teixeira 2) is a treasure trove of Portuguese music,
from fado to classical and contemporary, as well as books and sheet
music. It also has internet access. For hand-painted Portuguese
ceramics try Sintra Bazar and A Esquina (both in Praça da República),
head to Almorábida (Rua Visconde de Monserrate 12–15) for lace,
and Casa Branca (Rua Consiglieri Pedroso 12) for linens and
embroidered silks.

TAKING A BREAK

There are several cafés in the Old Town area, including by the station
and tram, in case you have to wait. Whilst in Sintra you should try a
queijada, a tasty local cake made from cheese, eggs, sugar, flour and
cinnamon.

A Piriquita £ ❶ Great for pastries. ⓐ Rua das Padarias 1–5 ⓣ 21 923
0626 ⓛ 08.00–19.00 Mon–Sun

Vila Velha £ ❷ Good for a quick snack. Stop by for a salad,
sandwich or *caldo verde*. It is located along the narrow alleyway

opposite the Palácio Nacional. ⓐ Rua das Padarias 8 ❶ 21 923 0154
🕐 08.00–19.00 Mon–Sun

Restaurants & bars

Tirol de Sintra £ ❸   A good basic place for lunch or dinner, this
restaurant has outdoor seating and serves traditional Portuguese
cuisine. Specialities include roast leg of lamb, pork meat with
clams, pizzas, homemade breads and local cheesecake (*queijada*).
ⓐ Avenida Heliodoro Salgado 5 ❶ 21 923 0505 🕐 07.00–22.00
Mon–Sun

Casa Orixás ££ ❹   This Brazilian restaurant has a choice of buffet
or à la carte menu with food from various regions, as well as tropical
gardens and lively ambience. ⓐ Avenida Adriano Julio Coelho 7
❶ 21 924 1672 🕐 16.00–24.00 Tues–Thur, until 01.00 Fri, 11.00–01.00
Sat, until 24.00 Sun ⓦ www.orixasclub.com

⬤ *Sintra's Castelo dos Mouros is a worthy reminder of Moorish style*

Cozinha Velha £££ ❺ Located in the former palace kitchen at the Palácio de Queluz (see page 135), this superb restaurant offers fine dining in luxurious surroundings. ⓐ Largo do Palácio ⓣ 21 435 6158 ⓛ 12.30–15.00 & 19.30–24.00 Mon–Sun

Restaurante Palácio Nacional da Pena £££ ❻ You can dine on traditional Portuguese cuisine at the restaurant inside the National Palace, but you will pay for the pleasure. ⓐ Estrada da Pena ⓣ 21 923 1208 ⓛ 12.00–16.00 & 19.00–24.00 Mon–Sun

ACCOMMODATION

Casal da Carregueira ££ Small guesthouse set in enclosed gardens near Queluz, dressed in period furniture with a bar, comfortable sitting room, sauna and barbecue area. ⓐ Belas ⓣ 21 432 1474 ⓦ www.portugalvirtual.pt

Hotel Tivoli Sintra ££ Located in the centre of Sintra, this hotel has a bar and restaurant with panoramic views of the valley. ⓐ Praça da República ⓣ 21 923 7200 ⓦ www.tivolihotels.com ⓔ htsintra@tivolihotels.com

Quinta de São Thiago ££ On the lower slopes of the Sintra hills, this 16th-century house has been modernised but has retained its chapel, old tiles, library and music room. There is also a swimming pool and tennis court. ⓐ Estrada de Monserrate ⓣ 21 923 2923 ⓦ www.portugalvirtual.pt

Hotel Tivoli Palácio de Seteais £££ Set in an 18th-century palace in the heart of the Serra de Sintra, this is a traditional hotel with period

🔺 *Unwind in the Parque do Estoril*

furniture and modern comforts, a bar and restaurant. ⓐ Avenida
Barbos du Bocage 8 ⓣ 21 923 3200 ⓦ www.tivolihotels.com
ⓔ htseteais@tivolihotels.com

Penha Longa Hotel & Golf Resort £££ Large resort hotel with
three restaurants, beautiful gardens, two golf courses, spa, health
club, indoor and outdoor pools, tennis courts and a jogging track.
ⓐ Estrada da Lagoa Azul, Linhó ⓣ 21 924 9007
ⓦ www.caesarparkpenhalonga.com ⓔ resort@penhalonga.com

Pousada de Queluz – Dona Maria I £££ Located by Queluz National
Palace, 5 km (3 miles) from Lisbon. Comfortable rooms with
mini-bar and satellite TV. ⓐ Largo do Palácio ⓣ 21 435 6158
ⓦ www.pousadas.pt ⓔ recepcao.dmaria@pousadas.pt

▶ *Find your way around with a street map*

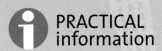

PRACTICAL
information

Directory

GETTING THERE

By air

Several airlines currently operate from the UK to Lisbon International Airport. British Airways operates four flights daily from London Heathrow, whilst TAP Portugal (the national airline) runs two flights daily from London Gatwick, and two or three from London Heathrow – both Monday to Saturday. Budget airline easyJet operates two flights daily from London Luton; Monarch runs one or two daily from London Gatwick; and Air Berlin offers one daily from London Stansted.

Air Berlin ☏ 0870 738 8880 ⓦ www.airberlin.com
British Airways ☏ 0870 850 9850 ⓦ www.ba.com
easyJet ☏ 0905 821 0905 ⓦ www.easyjet.co.uk
Monarch ☏ 0871 225 3555 ⓦ www.flymonarch.com
TAP Portugal ☏ 0845 241 7437 ⓦ www.flytap.com

Many people are aware that air travel emits CO_2, which contributes to climate change. You may be interested in the possibility of lessening the environmental impact of your flight through the charity Climate Care, which offsets your CO_2 by funding environmental projects around the world. Visit www.climatecare.org

By rail

To reach Lisbon by rail you will have to be prepared for a long haul and a few changes, but this might be an option if you are buying a multi-country train pass with stops along the way. From London you can take one of the frequent Eurostar services to Paris' Gare du Nord station. From there you should transfer to Paris Montparnasse and take a train to Irún (Gipuzkoa in Basque) in the Basque Country (Spain), and change again for a train directly to Lisboa Oriente (Parque das Nações). It takes at least 24 hours to do the journey non-stop. See ⓦ www.railpass.com for exact connections and tickets.

Eurostar ☎ 0870 442 8951 ⓦ www.eurostar.com
TGV ⓦ www.tgv.com
Renfe ⓦ www.renfe.es

ENTRY FORMALITIES
Visa requirements
People from EU countries can enter Portugal with either a valid identity card or passport. Citizens of Canada, the United States, Australia and New Zealand must travel with their passport but do not need a visa if staying for less than 90 days. Citizens of South Africa require a visa.

Customs
Travellers to Portugal are entitled to bring the following duty-paid goods into the country for their own personal use: up to 800 cigarettes, 10 litres of spirits, 90 litres of wine (60 litres of sparkling wine), and 110 litres of beer. However, if you are questioned by Customs officials and cannot satisfy them that it is not for commercial use, it could be seized and not returned.

If you are travelling to and from non-EU countries, you still have a duty-free allowance of 200 cigarettes or 50 cigars or 250 g of tobacco; 2 litres of wine or 1 litre of spirits; plus 50 g of perfume; 250 ml of eau de toilette; and gifts worth up to 50 euros.

MONEY

Portugal adopted the euro in 2002, and its former currency, the escudo, was withdrawn from circulation. Euro notes are available in denominations of 5, 10, 20, 50, 100, 200 and 500 euros; coins are available in 1, 2, 5, 10, 20 and 50 cents plus 1 and 2 euros. One side of the coin is common throughout the EU but the flipside is individual to the country where it was minted. However, all currency can be used throughout the EU countries where the euro is used.

You can change money and traveller's cheques, but be prepared to pay a commission – traveller's cheques should be in US dollars, pounds sterling or euros. However, with so many ATMs around, it is more likely that you will prefer to withdraw money as and when you need it. Most cards are accepted and the instructions are multilingual. Credit cards are also accepted at most places.

HEALTH, SAFETY & CRIME

Any public hospital can provide you with emergency treatment. Call 112 for emergencies or if you don't have anyone to take you. Please note that the former E111 is no longer valid. As part of a reciprocal agreement, citizens of the EU are entitled to reduced-cost and sometimes free medical treatment if they have a European Health Insurance Card (EHIC). You can apply for this online from the UK Department of Health (ⓦ www.dh.gov.uk) or by calling ⓣ 0845 606 2030. The card lasts for three to five years and covers medical treatment in the case of emergency or accident. Also make sure you take ID with you as well as your EHIC.

As this may not cover all your medical needs it is better to have your own private travel insurance to pay for repatriation, should you need it. Insurance also usually covers you if you are a victim of crime, but check your policy carefully before you travel.

Although Lisbon does not have a high crime rate compared with some cities, there has been a rise in violent crime in the past couple of decades. In general, Lisbon is safe, but tourists are easy targets for opportunists. Watch out for pickpockets in crowded areas, particularly where there is a high concentration of tourists, such as on tram No. 28. Be careful when travelling back to your hotel late at night, particularly in the dark, narrow streets of the Alfama, Bairro Alto and Chiado. If you are unlucky enough to be the victim of a crime, contact the tourist police in Praça dos Restauradores (☎ 21 342 1634). For lost property, ask the tourist police where you can find the nearest GNR (Guardia Nacional da República – National Guard).

OPENING HOURS

Most shops tend to open from 09.00–13.00 and 15.00–19.00 Mon–Fri. On Saturday some shops only open from 09.00–13.00. However, the large shopping centres are open from 09.00–24.00. Banking hours are generally 08.30–15.00 Mon–Fri, but some branches in Lisbon reopen from 18.00–23.00. Most museums open from 10.00–18.00 Tues–Sun, but this can vary – some also close for lunch.

TOILETS

There are public toilets in shopping centres, department stores, such as El Corte Inglés, and most museums. There are also toilets in the main railway stations. Cafés and bars have toilets but it is always better and more polite to buy something first.

CHILDREN

Most Portuguese are very good with children, and families regularly go out together to eat in the evening, even late at night. Children are welcome in most places except late-night bars and clubs. Depending on the age of the children, some museums and historic attractions might not be exciting enough for them. They might like to climb up the towers of the Castelo de São Jorge, the Torre de Belém and ride on the trams and elevators. Parque das Nações has various suitable attractions, including the Pavilhão de Conhecimento, the Oceanário, Torre Vasco da Gama and the Teleférico. There are various activities for children in the Parque Florestal de Monsanto, and the beaches of the Estoril coastline are also close enough to take a day trip. They are easily reached by train from Cais do Sodré. Other attractions and activities for children include:

- **Lisboa Zoo** There is a wide range of animals at the zoo from big cats and camels to tropical birds and reptiles. Feeding time is a good time to take the children, and there are numerous rides as well. ⓐ Estrada de Benfica ⓣ 21 723 2900 ⓦ www.zoolisboa.pt ⓛ 10.00–18.00

- **Playgrounds** There are several playgrounds in the Parque das Nações, including: Jumicar (Sony Plaza) where children over 7 years can learn to drive real, environmentally friendly, junior-sized cars; Micolandia (Sony Plaza), a playground with inflatable equipment such as a castle, slides, tunnels and mazes; Music Playground (Passeio das Tágides) with various giant instruments for the children to jump on or hit to make a sound; and Parque do Tejo Playground and Pyrâmide do Gil Playground (Tagus Gardens) where children can climb on various wooden animals, a climbing wall and frames.

- **Tejo Bike** You can hire bicycles in the Parque das Nações – there are many safe routes here. There is a discount of 20 per cent if you

have a park card (see page 113). ⓐ Rossio dos Olivais or Sony Plaza
ⓣ 21 891 9333 ⓔ tejobike@iol.pt

- **Tourist Mini Train** This small train travels round the Parque das
  Nações and is included in the park card (see page 113). The route
  begins and ends at Alameda dos Oceanos in front of the Pavilhão
  Atlântico. ⓐ Parque das Nações ⓣ 21 358 2334

COMMUNICATIONS
Phones
Many people prefer to take their mobile phones abroad these days
rather than using a public phone. Before you go remember to
contact your mobile provider to make sure your phone is activated
for international use. Also check that your existing handset will
work in Portugal and how much the charges for calls and texts will
be. You will often have to pay for receiving calls whilst roaming and
texts can be charged twice, depending on the provider. Phone
providers in Portugal include Vodafone, Optimus and TSM.

Telephones in hotels are also convenient but tend to be quite
expensive for anything other than a local call. Charges should be
provided in your room. If they aren't, ask at reception.

Using a public telephone box is quite easy, and direct dialling in
Lisbon is not a problem. Public phones can be found in cafés and
bars as well as stations and in the street. Phones take euro coins in
denominations of 2 cents up to 2 euros. Alternatively, phone cards
can be bought from newspaper kiosks, the post office or other retail
outlets – ask for a CrediPhone – and they come in units of 50, 100 or
150. To call abroad, dial 00 then the country code and city/local code,
minus the first 0. You can also make calls at post offices and pay for
the call at the end.

Post

Post office (*correios* ⓦ www.ctt.com) opening times can vary in the larger cities. The main post offices in Lisbon, Cascais, Estoril and Sintra can be found at:

ⓐ Praça dos Restauradores, Lisbon ⓛ 08.00–22.00

ⓐ Aeroporto, Lisbon ⓛ 24 hours

ⓐ Avenida Marginal, Lote C, Cascais ⓛ 09.00–18.00

ⓐ Avenida Nice 1, Estoril ⓛ 09.30–19.30

ⓐ Praça D Afonso Henriques 7 ⓛ 08.30–18.00

Internet

Internet cafés include:

Cyberstore ⓐ Rua Nova do Almada 105–115, Chiado
ⓦ www.cyberchiado.com ⓛ 10.00–22.00

Lisbon Welcome Centre ⓐ Praça do Comércio ⓣ 21 346 3314
ⓛ 09.00–20.00

Net Centre Café ⓐ Rua Diário de Noticias ⓛ 16.00–02.00

Peter Café Sport ⓐ Rua da Pimenta, Parque das Nações ⓛ 11.00–01.00

ELECTRICITY

The voltage is 220/380 volts at a frequency of 50 hertz. Plug sockets follow European standards. To use American-type plugs, a 220-volt transformer should be used, together with an adapter plug.

TRAVELLERS WITH DISABILITIES

Access for travellers with disabilities is improving in Portugal, in line with EU regulations. There are toilet facilities, lifts on the metro and ramps in modern buildings. At the airport, wheelchairs can be provided and staff can help wheelchair passengers through customs and immigration. You need to request help when you book your ticket. There are also disabled parking spaces and two lifts to take passengers to different levels.

FURTHER INFORMATION
Lisbon tourist offices
There are three main tourist offices in Lisbon:

ⓐ Airport ☎ 21 845 0660 ⏰ 08.00–24.00. Located in the main arrivals hall, use this kiosk to ask for immediate information on accommodation, maps and main attractions. You also need to go here to pick up a taxi voucher into the city centre.

ⓐ Palácio Foz, Praça dos Restauradores ☎ 21 346 3314 ⏰ 09.00–20.00. You can pick up information here and there is also a shop.

ⓐ Praça do Comércio ☎ 21 346 3314 ⏰ 09.00–20.00. This is the main tourist office, the Lisbon Welcome Centre, and provides detailed information on accommodation, attractions, tours, discount cards and travel cards. It also has a café, internet access and a shop.

Websites
Lisbon
Lisbon's tourist office website covers both the city as well as Estoril, Leiria/Fatima, Costa Azul, Sintra, Templarios, Oeste, Ribatejo and other places close by. ⓦ www.atl-turismolisboa.pt

The Lisbon local authority website also has a good tourist information section. ⓦ www.cm-lisboa.pt

Estoril/Cascais

The Estoril Coast Tourism website covers the region west of
Oeiras and south of Sintra, and includes Estoril and Cascais,
as well as various coastal and inland towns and villages.
Ⓦ www.estorilcoast-tourism.com

Sintra

Sintra's local authority website covers all aspects of tourism and
culture in the area. Ⓦ www.cm-sintra.pt

Background reading

Lisbon by Paul Buck gives an interesting insight into the city.
A cultural and literary companion, the book provides factual
information on the city's history and sights, often through the views
of artists and writers.

The Last Kabbalist of Lisbon by Richard Zimmler is a crime thriller set
in the 16th century during the time of Jewish persecution. Following
the style of *The Name of the Rose*, which blurs the lines between
fiction and history, a manuscript is discovered hidden in a cellar in
Turkey. These manuscripts reveal the search by a young kabbalist,
Berekiah Zarco, for clues to the murder of his uncle in the Alfama.

For some local literature try José Saramago (*Baltasar and Blimunda*,
The History of the Siege of Lisbon, *Journey to Portugal: In Pursuit of
Portugal's History and Culture*, *The Year of the Death of Ricardo Reis*) or
Fernando Pessoa (*The Book of Disquiet*, *Poems of Fernando Pessoa*).

▶ *The garish Palácio da Pena in Sintra*

Useful phrases

Although English is widely spoken in Portugal, these words and phrases may come in handy. See also the phrases for specific situations in other parts of the book.

English	Portuguese	Approx. pronunciation
BASICS		
Yes	Sim	Seem
No	Não	Nown
Please	Por favor	Poor favohr
Thank you	Obrigado/a	Ohbreegahdoo/a
Hello	Olá	Ohlah
Goodbye	Adeus	Adayoosh
Excuse me	Com licença	Cong lisensah
Sorry	Desculpe	Dishkoolper
That's okay	Está bem	Istah bayng
To	Para	Para
From	De	Di
I don't speak Portuguese	Não sei falar Português	Nown say falahr Portoogehsh
Do you speak English?	Fala Inglês?	Fahla eenglaysh?
Good morning	Bom día	Bohm deea
Good afternoon	Boa tarde	Boha tahrd
Good evening	Boa noite	Boha noyt
Goodnight	Boa noite	Boha noyt
My name is ...	Chamo-me ...	Shamoo-mi ...
DAYS & TIMES		
Monday	Segunda-feira	Sigoongda-fayra
Tuesday	Terça-feira	Tayrsa-fayra
Wednesday	Quarta-feira	Kwahrta-fayra
Thursday	Quinta-feira	Keengta-fayra
Friday	Sexta-feira	Sayshta-fayra
Saturday	Sábado	Sahbadoo
Sunday	Domingo	Doomeengoo
Morning	Manhã	Manyang
Afternoon	Tarde	Tahrd
Evening	Noite	Noyt
Night	Noite	Noyt
Yesterday	Ontem	Ohngtayng

English	Portuguese	*Approx. pronunciation*
Today	Hoje	*Ohzhay*
Tomorrow	Amanhã	*Ahmanyang*
What time is it?	Que horas são?	*Ki orash sowng?*
It is ...	É/São ...	*Eh/Sowng ...*
09.00	Nove horas	*Nov orash*
Midday/Midnight	Meio dia/Meia noite	*Mayoo-deea/Maya-noyt*

NUMBERS

One	Um	*Oong*
Two	Dois	*Doysh*
Three	Três	*Traysh*
Four	Quatro	*Kwahtroo*
Five	Cinco	*Seengkoo*
Six	Seis	*Saysh*
Seven	Sete	*Set*
Eight	Oito	*Oytoo*
Nine	Nove	*Nov*
Ten	Dez	*Desh*
Eleven	Onze	*Ohngz*
Twelve	Doze	*Dohz*
Twenty	Vinte	*Veengt*
Fifty	Cinquenta	*Seengkwayngta*
One hundred	Cem	*Sayng*

MONEY

I would like to change these traveller's cheques/this currency	Queria trocar estes cheques de viagem/ estas divisas	*Kireea trookahr aystsh shehkish di veeazhayng/ ehshtash deeveezash*
Where is the nearest ATM?	Onde fica a caixa multibanco mais próxima?	*Awngder feeka ah kysha moltibahngkoo mysh prossima?*
Do you accept traveller's cheques/credit cards?	Aceita cheques de viagem/cartões de crédito?	*Asayta shehkiesh di veeahzhayng/kartoyesh di kredeetoo?*

SIGNS & NOTICES

Airport	Aeroporto	*Aehrohpootoo*
Rail station/Platform	Estação de Caminho de Férro/Linha	*Ishtasowng di kamihnyo di fehrroo/ Leenya*
Smoking/ Non-smoking	Fumadores/ Não fumadores	*Foomadohrsh/ Nown-foomadohrsh*
Toilets	Lavabos	*Lavahboosh*
Ladies/Gentlemen	Senhoras/Homens (Cavalheiros)	*Sinyohrash/Omayngsh (Kavalyayroosh)*
Subway	Metropolitano	*Metropooleetahnoo*

Emergencies

EMERGENCY NUMBERS

For police, ambulance and fire services, the number is 112

MEDICAL EMERGENCIES

In an emergency you should go to the nearest public hospital, which will provide emergency treatment. EU citizens with an EHIC are entitled to reduced-cost, and sometimes free, basic treatment (make sure you take ID with you as well as your EHIC). It is always better to have medical insurance though, even if you have an EHIC, for any unforeseen costs, and essential if you are a non-EU visitor.

If you can get to a hospital yourself, head for *urgências* or a 24-hour public health clinic. Pharmacies (*farmacia*) can help you with a list of emergency clinics, doctors and dentists.

Hospital Santa Maria ⓐ Avda Prof Egas Moniz ⓣ 21 780 5000; Urgencias: 21 780 5111 and 21 780 5222

British Hospital ⓐ Rua Saraiva de Carvalho 49 ⓣ 21 394 3133

Clinica Internacional de Saúde de Cascais ⓐ Rua João Infante, Lote 1 r/c A, Alto das Flores, Bairro do Rosario, Cascais ⓣ 21 486 5946

Doctors

Dr David Ernst ⓐ Clínica Médica Internacional de Lisboa, Avenida António Augusto Aguiar ⓣ 21 351 3310

Dr Andrew French ⓐ International Health Centre, Rua do Regimento Dezanove 67, 2nd floor ⓣ 21 484 5318

Dentists

Dr Francis Haley B.D.S. and Dr D B Skinner ⓐ Avenida 25 de Abril, Edificio Grei 184, 1st floor, Cascais ⓣ 21 486 3011

Dr R Kristensen ⓐ Clínica Dentária Prodan, Rua Arco do Carvalhão
Lda 24 ⓘ 21 383 2174

POLICE

The tourist police are located in Praça dos Restauradores (ⓘ 21 342
1634). For lost property, find the nearest GNR (Guardia Nacional da
República – National Guard).

CONSULATES & EMBASSIES

Australian Embassy ⓐ Avenida da Liberdade 198, 2nd floor
ⓘ 21 310 1500 ⓦ www.portugal.embassy.gov.au
Canadian Embassy ⓐ Avenida da Liberdade 196–200, 3rd floor
ⓘ 21 316 4600 ⓦ www.portugal.gc.ca
Irish Embassy ⓐ Rua Imprensa-Estrela 1, 4th floor ⓘ 21 392 9440
New Zealand Consulate ⓐ Rua da Vista Alegre 10 ⓘ 21 370 5870
South African Embassy ⓐ São Sebastião de Pedreira, Avenida Luís
Bívar 10 ⓘ 21 319 2200
UK Embassy ⓐ Rua de São Bernardo 33, Lisbon ⓘ 21 392 40 00
ⓦ www.uk-embassy.pt
US Embassy ⓐ Avenida das Forcas Armadas ⓘ 21 727 3300
ⓦ lisbon.usembassy.gov/

EMERGENCY PHRASES
Help! Socorro! *Sookohrroo!* **Fire!** Fogo! *Fohgoo!*
Stop! Pare! *Pahreh!*
Call an ambulance/a doctor/the police/the fire brigade!
Chame uma ambulância/um médico/a polícia/os bombeiros!
*Shami ooma angboolangsya/oong medeekoo/a
pooleesseeya/oosh bombehroosh!*

INDEX

The publishers would like to thank the following photographers for supplying the copyright photographs for this book:

Alan Grant: page 153; Pictures Colour Library: pages 61 and 68; Robert Harding World Imagery: page 112;
Christopher Holt: all other photographs

Copy editor: Jenni Rainford
Proofreader: Janet McCann

Send your thoughts to
books@thomascook.com

- **Found a great bar, club, shop or must-see sight that we don't feature?**

- **Like to tip us off about any information that needs updating?**

- **Want to tell us what you love about this handy little guidebook and more importantly how we can make it even handier?**

Then here's your chance to tell all! Send us ideas, discoveries and recommendations today and then look out for your valuable input in the next edition of this title. As an extra 'thank you' from Thomas Cook Publishing, you'll be automatically entered into our exciting monthly prize draw.

Send an email to the above address (stating the book's title) or write to: CitySpots Project Editor, Thomas Cook Publishing, PO Box 227, The Thomas Cook Business Park, Unit 18, Coningsby Road, Peterborough PE3 8SB, UK.